Modification of Position and Attitude Determination of a Test Article Through Photogrammetry to Account for Structural Deformation

Air Force Institute of Technology (U.S.). Graduate School of Engineering and Management, Anonymous

MODIFICATION OF POSITION AND ATTITUDE DETERMINATION OF A TEST ARTICLE THROUGH PHOTOGRAMMETRY TO ACCOUNT FOR STRUCTURAL DEFORMATION

THESIS

Sean A. Krolikowski, First Lieutenant, USAF

AFIT/GA/ENY/01M-03

DEPARTMENT OF THE AIR FORCE
AIR UNIVERSITY

AIR FORCE INSTITUTE OF TECHNOLOGY

Wright-Patterson Air Force Base, Ohio

APPROVED FOR PUBLIC RELEASE; DISTRIBUTION UNLIMITED

The views expressed in this thesis are those of the author and do not reflect the official policy or position of the United States Air Force, Department of Defense, or the United States Government.

AFIT/GA/ENY/01M-3

MODIFICATION OF POSITION AND ATTITUDE DETERMINATION OF A TEST ARTICLE THROUGH PHOTOGRAMMETRY TO ACCOUNT FOR STRUCTURAL DEFORMATION

THESIS

Presented to the Faculty

Department of Aeronautics and Astronautics

Graduate School of Engineering and Management

Air Force Institute of Technology

Air University

Air Eductaion and Training Command

in Partial Fulfillment of the Requirements for the

Degree of Master of Science in Astronautical Engineering

Sean Andrew Krolikowski, B.S.

First Lieutenant, USAF

March 2001

APPROVED FOR PUBLIC RELEASE; DISTRIBUTION UNLIMITED

AFIT/GA/ENY/01M-03

MODIFICATION OF POSITION AND ATTITUDE DETERMINATION OF A TEST ARTICLE THROUGH PHOTOGRAMMETRY TO ACCOUNT FOR STRUCTURAL DEFORMATION

Sean Andrew Krolikowski, B.S.

First Lieutenant, USAF

Approved:

_____   7 MAR 01
Dr. Steven Tragesser (Chairman)   Date

_____   7 March 01
Dr. Curtis Spenny (Member)   Date

_____   7 MAR 01
Maj Montgomery Hughson (Member)   Date

Acknowledgements

I would like to thank my advisor, Dr. Steven Tragesser, for all of his help on this thesis. I would also like to thank Dr. Wim Ruyten for his guidance and for providing the code for the rigid model which I modified to include deformation. If I had to start from scratch I think I would still be coding. Finally, I would like to thank my fiancee, for all of her love and support, even if it was from the other side of the country.

Sean Andrew Krolikowski

Table of Contents

	Page
Acknowledgements	iv
List of Figures	vii
List of Symbols	viii
List of Abbreviations	ix
Abstract	x

I.	Introduction	1-1
	1.1 Background	1-1
	1.2 Problem Statement	1-2
	1.3 Methodology	1-2
	1.4 Assumptions/Limitations	1-3
II.	Position and Attitude Determination	2-1
	2.1 Non-Topographic Photogrammetry	2-1
	2.2 Nonlinear Fitting Scheme	2-5
	2.3 Levenberg-Marquardt	2-8
III.	Deformation Modeling	3-1
	3.1 Parabolic Bending	3-1
	3.2 Linear Twist	3-4
	3.3 Implementaion of Deformation Models	3-6
	3.4 Evaluating the Deformation Model	3-9
	3.4.1 Target Distribution	3-10
	3.4.2 Camera Views	3-11

			Page
IV.	Results	. . . .	4-1
V.	Conclusions	. . . .	5-1
Appendix A.	MATLAB Code	. . . .	A-1
Appendix B.	Fortran Code	. . . .	B-1
Appendix C.	Data Runs	. . . .	C-1
C.1	Runs Varying Number of Data Points	. . . .	C-1
C.2	Runs Varying Number of Cameras	. . . .	C-3
C.3	Runs Varying Bending Coefficient	. . . .	C-7
C.4	Runs Varying Twisting Coefficient	. . . .	C-9
C.5	Runs Varying Noise	. . . .	C-12
Bibliography	. . . .	BIB-1
Vita	. . . .	VITA-1

List of Figures

Figure		Page
2.1.	NTP Set Up	2-2
2.2.	Wind Tunnel Set Up	2-5
3.1.	Parabolic Bending Set Up	3-1
3.2.	Wire-frame Bent Wing	3-2
3.3.	Linear Twisting Set Up	3-4
3.4.	Wire-Frame Twisted Wing	3-5
3.5.	Set-up of Truth Model Test Article	3-9
3.6.	Set-Up of Y Interval Determination	3-11
3.7.	Wind Tunnel Camera Set Up	3-12
3.8.	Sample View of Cameras 1-4	3-13
3.9.	Sample View of Cameras 5-8	3-13
4.1.	Relative Error Versus Number of Data Points, Severely Deformed	4-1
4.2.	Relative Error Versus Number of Data Points, Moderately Deformed	4-2
4.3.	Relative Error Versus YCF	4-3
4.4.	Comparison of YCF=1 to YCF=1.25	4-4
4.5.	Relative error versus number of cameras, moderate bending	4-4
4.6.	Relative Error Versus Number of Cameras, Severe bending	4-5
4.7.	Relative Error Versus Bending Coefficient for Bending and Rigid Models	4-6
4.8.	Relative Error Versus Twisting Coefficient for Bending and Rigid Models	4-7
4.9.	Relative Error Versus Noise Level for Bending and Rigid Models	4-8

List of Symbols

Symbol	Page
f Focal Length	2-1
$\vec{A}$ vector from f to target on model	2-1
$\vec{a}$ vector from f to target in image	2-2
ϕ roll angle of model	2-5
α pitch angle of model	2-5
β yaw angle of model	2-5
Δx displacement of model frame from tunnel frame in x direction	2-6
Δy displacement of model frame from tunnel frame in x direction	2-6
Δz displacement of model frame from tunnel frame in x direction	2-6
$\vec{q}$ unknown parameter vector	2-7
χ^2 merit function	2-7
K_{bend} bending coefficient	3-2
L length of wing	3-2
K_{twist} twisting coefficient	3-5
XDF X Density Factor	3-10
YDF Y Density Factor	3-10
YCF Y Cluster Factor	3-10

List of Abbreviations

Abbreviation	Page
L-M Levenberg-Marquardt	x
AEDC Arnold Engineering Development Center	1-1
PSP Pressure-Sensitive Paint	1-1
NTP Non-Topographic Photogrammetry	2-1
TRS Tunnel Reference System	2-5
rms Root Mean Squared	2-8

AFIT/GA/ENY/01M-3

Abstract

The Arnold Engineering Development Center (AEDC) at Arnold AFB, TN currently has a computer program which, through a process known as photogrammetry, combines multiple 2D images of a wind tunnel test article, affixed with numerous registration markers, and the known 3D coordinates of those markers. It can then accurately determine the unknown position and attitude of the test article relative to the wind tunnel. The current algorithm has a problem in that it assumes the test article is a rigid body, when, in fact, the test article experiences deformation under aerodynamic loads. Due to this deformation, the 3D coordinates of the markers are not precisely known.

This research looks at modifying the current program to account for this deformation and to improve the accuracy of the position and attitude determination of the test article. The current program uses the Levenberg-Marquardt method of multi-parameter optimization to solve for the unknown parameters of position and attitude. In this work, deformation is modeled in two modes, simple parabolic bending and linear twisting, and uses the L-M method to solve for these additional parameters. This work also determines the minimum number of targets and cameras required to obtain the maximum accuracy. It varies the model targets from about 20 to 200, and looks at using 1, 2, 4, 6, and 8 cameras. The results are a great improvement in accuracy over the original program. The results also show that optimal accuracy is obtained with approximately 50 targets and 2 cameras. Any more than this produces an extremely small improvement in accuracy, with no real added benefit.

It is clear that by adding simple bending and twisting parameters to the list of unknowns in the L-M solver, a much greater accuracy can be achieved in the determination of the position and attitude.

MODIFICATION OF POSITION AND ATTITUDE DETERMINATION OF A TEST ARTICLE THROUGH PHOTOGRAMMETRY TO ACCOUNT FOR STRUCTURAL DEFORMATION

I. Introduction

1.1 Background

One of the tasks of the Arnold Engineering Development Center (AEDC) at Arnold Air Force Base, Tennessee is to place the customer's small-scale model of their vehicle, be it airplane, heavy lift rocket, etc., in a wind tunnel and measure the aerodynamic loading, giving an approximation of what the real loading environment will be. The old method was to use a "a pressure loads model, one instrumented with hundreds of pressure orifices" [8] to measure the pressures across the model's surface. Today that method is changing to one that is more efficient and cost-effective. That method utilizes pressure-sensitive paint PSP. Dr. Wim Ruyten, AEDC, describes this process [10]:

> In PSP measurements, we paint scale models of aircraft or other objects with a special paint that glows when ultraviolet light shines on it. The glow has a different color than the light that produces it, so we can use optical filters to separate the two. Even more important, the brightness of the glow depends on the air pressure on the model. So by taking pictures of the model, we can back out what the pressure is.

A crucial element of the pressure determination process is knowing the exact position and attitude of the test article relative to the wind tunnel. In the old method, this was done with "a complex procedure for combining and calibrating data from sting-mounted balance sensors and strain gages." [5] Dr. Ruyten goes on the say that "...there is a growing interest to measure angles of attack with an accuracy that surpasses .01 deg. This level of accuracy cannot be obtained using traditional measurements based on balance sensors and strain gages." [6] Once again, a more accurate and efficient method was found. It is an optical method using registration markers placed on the test article. Through a process known as photogrammetry, it is possible to take one or more 2D images of the article and it's registration markers, or targets, and combine that with the known 3D coordinates of the targets to back out the position and attitude of the article.

There is a problem with the current method. This method assumes that the test article is a rigid body. This mean that the three-dimensional coordinates of the targets in the model reference frame are known at all times. This is not the case. After repeated exposure to aerodynamic loading, the article, notably appendages such as wings and stabilizers, will experience small structural deformations. This means that the three-dimensional coordinates of the targets in the model frame are constantly changing. As time progresses and the model becomes more deformed, the current method will become more and more inaccurate at position and attitude determination.

1.2 Problem Statement

Improve the accuracy of position and attitude determination of a wind tunnel test article by accounting for structural deformation. Determine the optimal number of targets and cameras needed to obtain the acceptable accuracy.

1.3 Methodology

The current method utilizes the Levenberg-Marquardt method of multi-parameter optimization. The known parameters are the camera location(s) and orientation(s) and the 3D coordinates of the registration markers in the model coordinate frame. The unknown parameters are the three position and three attitude parameters. It then minimizes the least squares merit function of the predicted target coordinates in the camera frame and the measured target coordinates in the camera frame. This minimization produces the six position and attitude parameters.

This thesis adds two unknown parameters to the equations, a parabolic bending coefficient and a linear twisting coefficient. By adding these simple models of deformation, the program will more accurately compute the position and attitude of a deformed test article.

This thesis also completes many sample runs of data, varying both the number of targets and the number of cameras. Through this analysis it shows that there is an optimal number of targets and cameras where the accuracy is still kept at a maximum.

1.4 Assumptions/Limitations

The methodology employed here tries to model the deformation of the test article in two ways, parabolic bending and linear twist about a central line. There are some limitations in this method which will prevent it from ever precisely determining the position and attitude of the article. First, this method was conceived with the assumption that the deformed piece of the article would be a wing or a rocket fin or some other protrusion from a main body. The idea of a second order bending and a first order twisting are suited to this type of application. The majority of AEDC's test articles are an aircraft configuration of some type, which is why this method is used. However, this method may not be appropriate for every conceivable test article that AEDC may use. Second, second order bending and first order twisting are very simple approximations of the true deformation that occurs. These are believed to be good approximations, but they are by no means perfect.

II. Position and Attitude Determination

2.1 Non-Topographic Photogrammetry

Accurate determination of position and attitude of the wind tunnel test article is not only important for pressure-sensitive paint testing, but is in fact "one of the persistent interests in wind tunnel testing" [6] Balance sensor and strain gages are not meeting todays accuracy requirements. More accurate optical methods are being used, and those methods are based on a method known as Non-Topographic Photogrammetry, introduced in 1979 by H.M. Karara et al. [2]

Non-Topographic Photogrammetry (NTP) considers the case where an object has been photographed by one or more exterior cameras. The goal is to determine the coordinates of the targets (small black dots placed on the surface of the test article) in the two dimensional frame of the photograph. The three dimensional coordinates of the targets in the model frame are assumed known, and the position and orientation of the camera(s) need to be determined through calibration. In this thesis, one of the assumptions is that the position and orientation of the camera(s) are already known, because the calibration process is performed before any aerodynamic loading is placed on the model, and thus the model remains undeformed. Therefore, the details of the calibration process will not be presented. It should also be noted that any lens or image distortion are neglected in this study, as the cameras are assumed to be perfect.

The configuration of object and camera can be seen in Figure 2.1. From the figure, $\widehat{XYZ}$ is the frame associated with the test article or model, and $\widehat{uv}$ is the frame associated with the photograph (hence the inverted image). The camera lens is at the intersection of all the lines, and is denoted by the focal length, f. For the derivation, we have selected one target point on the top of the canopy, denoted by (x_i, y_i, z_i). $\vec{A}$ is the vector from the focal point to the selected target point on

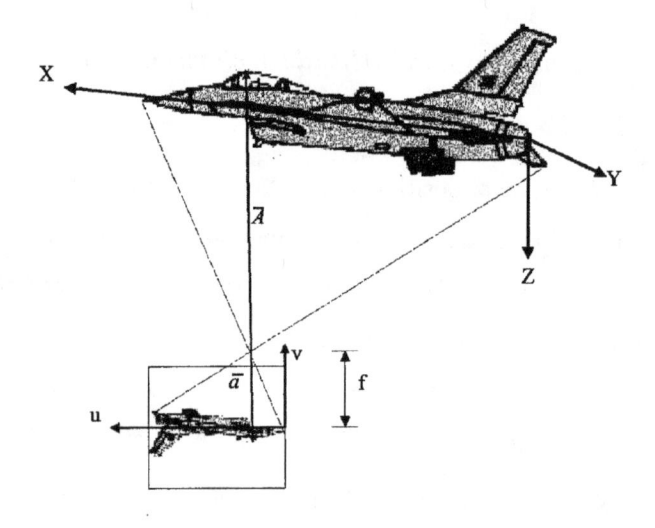

Figure 2.1   NTP Set Up

the model. $\vec{a}$ is the vector from the focal point to the selected target point in the photographic image, denoted by (u_i, v_i)

The relationship between the model frame and the image frame needs to be established. This relationship can be described by a three axis coordinate transformation. First, the model frame is rotated about it's X axis by an angle ω, arriving at the first intermediary axis. This axis is then rotated about it's Y' axis by an angle ϕ, taking it to the second intermediary axis. Finally, this axis can be rotated about it's Z'' axis by an angle κ, transforming it into the final image coordinate frame.

$$\begin{bmatrix} X' \\ Y' \\ Z' \end{bmatrix} = \begin{bmatrix} 1 & 0 & 0 \\ 0 & \cos\omega & \sin\omega \\ 0 & -\sin\omega & \cos\omega \end{bmatrix} \begin{bmatrix} X \\ Y \\ Z \end{bmatrix} \qquad (2.1)$$

$$\begin{bmatrix} X'' \\ Y'' \\ Z'' \end{bmatrix} = \begin{bmatrix} \cos\phi & 0 & -\sin\phi \\ 0 & 1 & 0 \\ \sin\phi & 0 & \cos\phi \end{bmatrix} \begin{bmatrix} X' \\ Y' \\ Z' \end{bmatrix} \qquad (2.2)$$

$$\begin{bmatrix} u \\ v \\ w \end{bmatrix} = \begin{bmatrix} \cos\kappa & \sin\kappa & 0 \\ -\sin\kappa & \cos\kappa & 0 \\ 0 & 0 & 1 \end{bmatrix} \begin{bmatrix} X'' \\ Y'' \\ Z'' \end{bmatrix} \quad (2.3)$$

Equations (2.1), (2.2), (2.3) can be combined to form one large transformation matrix, Equation (2.4).

$$M = \begin{bmatrix} \cos\kappa\cos\phi & \cos\kappa\sin\phi\sin\omega + \sin\kappa\cos\omega & -\cos\kappa\sin\phi\cos\omega + \sin\kappa\sin\omega \\ -\sin\kappa\cos\phi & -\sin\kappa\sin\phi\sin\omega + \cos\kappa\cos\omega & \sin\kappa\sin\phi\cos\omega + \cos\kappa\sin\omega \\ \sin\phi & -\cos\phi\sin\omega & \cos\phi\cos\omega \end{bmatrix} \quad (2.4)$$

The focal point is given coordinates in both reference frames. In the model frame it is denoted as (x_c, y_c, z_c). In the image frame, the focal coordinates are (u_c, v_c). Thus $\vec{A}$ now becomes Equation (2.5), and $\vec{a}$ now becomes Equation (2.6).

$$\vec{A} = \begin{bmatrix} x_i - x_c \\ y_i - y_c \\ z_i - z_c \end{bmatrix} \quad (2.5)$$

$$\vec{a} = \begin{bmatrix} u_i - u_c \\ v_i - v_c \\ -f \end{bmatrix} \quad (2.6)$$

To compare the two vectors $\vec{a}$ and $\vec{A}$, we need to get them both in terms of coordinates in the same reference frame. Thus, M will transform $\vec{A}$ to the image coordinate frame. The result is shown below where U, V, and W are the coordinates of $\vec{A}$ in the image frame.

$$U = (\cos\kappa\cos\phi)(x_i - x_c) + (\cos\kappa\sin\phi\sin\omega + \sin\kappa\cos\omega)(y_i - y_c)$$
$$+ (-\cos\kappa\sin\phi\cos\omega + \sin\kappa\sin\omega)(z_i - z_c)$$

$$V = (-\sin\kappa\cos\phi)(x_i - x_c) + (-\sin\kappa\sin\phi\sin\omega + \cos\kappa\cos\omega)(y_i - y_c) \quad (2.7)$$
$$+ (\sin\kappa\sin\phi\cos\omega + \cos\kappa\sin\omega)(z_i - z_c)$$
$$W = (\sin\phi)(x_i - x_c) + (-\cos\phi\sin\omega)(y_i - y_c) + (\cos\phi\cos\omega)(z_i - z_c)$$

The key to this whole process is realizing that, due to the nature of imaging, $\vec{A}$ and $\vec{a}$ are collinear. As H.M. Karara says, "The imaging process requires that the image and object rays be collinear, that is, that the components of the two vectors expressed in the same coordinate system be equal, except for a scale factor." [2] Thus we can say that $\vec{a} = kM\vec{A}$, where k is the scale factor. Expressing this equation in the image frame coordinates, we get

$$u_i - u_c = kU$$
$$v_i - v_c = kV \quad (2.8)$$
$$-f = kW$$

The exact value of the scale factor k is unknown, but we can solve the third equation of (2.8) for k, and substitute that result into the first and second equations of (2.8). This gives us equation (2.9).

$$u_i = u_c - f\frac{U}{W}$$
$$v_i = v_c - f\frac{V}{W} \quad (2.9)$$

This is the result of Non-Topographic Photogrammetry. Knowing the location of the camera lens (or focus), the coordinates of the desired target in the model frame, and the orientation of the model frame with respect to the image frame, we can calculate what the coordinates of that target will be in the image frame. Position and attitude determination will turn this around and, knowing what the image coordinates of the target are from the image taken, determine what the orientation of the model is with respect to the camera.

2.2 Nonlinear Fitting Scheme

Non-Topographic Photogrammetry can now be applied to the test article in the wind tunnel to determine the position and orientation of the article with respect to the tunnel. The initial set up can be seen in Figure 2.2, where $\widehat{XYZ}^*$ is the coordinate frame associated with the tunnel, also known as the Tunnel Reference System or TRS.

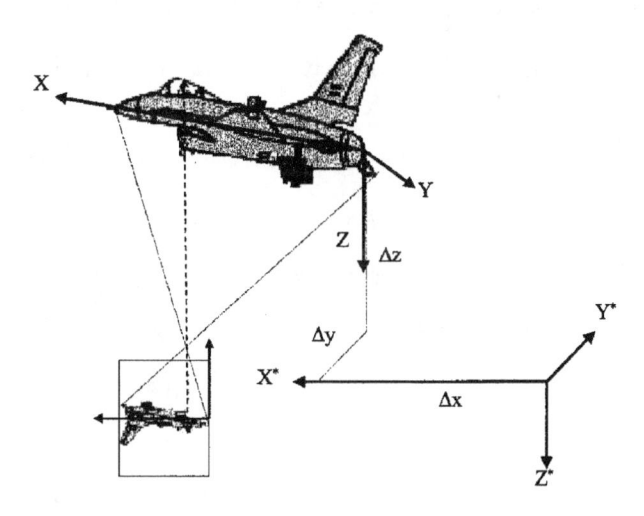

Figure 2.2   Wind Tunnel Set Up

The TRS and the model frame may be offset by three Euler angles. A rotation about the X^* axis will be denoted by ϕ, and is also known as roll. A rotation about the Y^* axis will be denoted by α, and is also known as pitch. A rotation about the Z^* axis will be denoted by β, and is also known as yaw. The first task is to transform the coordinates of the target from the model frame to the tunnel frame. This is accomplished in Equation (2.10), which shows that this is just a matter of rotating the model frame to the tunnel frame, similar to what was done in the previous section, but R is the rotation matrix using the angles α, β, and ϕ, whereas M was the rotation matrix using the angles κ, ϕ, and ω. Also, the displacements of the model frame from the tunnel frame, Δx, Δy, and Δz have been added in.

$$x_i^* = \Delta x + M x_i$$
$$y_i^* = \Delta y + M y_i \qquad (2.10)$$
$$z_i^* = \Delta z + M z_i$$

Where x_i, y_i, and z_i are the coordinates of the target point in the model frame, and x_i^*, y_i^*, and z_i^* are the coordinates of the target point in the tunnel reference frame.

The coordinates of the target in the TRS are given by Equation (2.11).

$$x_i^* = \Delta x + x_i(\cos\alpha\cos\beta) + y_i(\sin\beta\cos\phi + \sin\alpha\cos\beta\sin\phi)$$
$$+ z_i(-\sin\beta\sin\phi + \sin\alpha\cos\beta\cos\phi)$$
$$y_i^* = \Delta y + x_i(-\cos\alpha\sin\beta) + y_i(\cos\beta\cos\phi - \sin\alpha\sin\beta\sin\phi) \qquad (2.11)$$
$$+ z_i(-\cos\beta\sin\phi - \sin\alpha\sin\beta\cos\phi)$$
$$z_i^* = \Delta z + x_i(-\sin\alpha) + y_i(\cos\alpha\sin\phi) + z_i(\cos\alpha\cos\phi)$$

It is assumed that both the camera location and orientation are known from calibration. The location and orientation parameters, instead of being with respect to the model frame as in the previous section, are here with respect to the TRS. The location parameters are given by x_c^*, y_c^*, and z_c^*. The orientation angles of the camera are given by ϕ_c^*, κ_c^*, and ω_c^*. The coordinates of the target are now transformed from the tunnel frame to the image frame, using the same camera rotation matrix as before. The coordinates in the image frame U, V, and W are now affixed with an asterisk to indicate that they came from tunnel coordinates. This is shown by

Equation 2.12.

$$U_{ci}^* = (\cos\kappa^* \cos\phi^*)(x_i^* - x_c^*) + (\cos\kappa^* \sin\phi^* \sin\omega^* + \sin\kappa^* \cos\omega^*)(y_i^* - y_c^*)$$
$$+ (-\cos\kappa^* \sin\phi^* \cos\omega^* + \sin\kappa^* \sin\omega^*)(z_i^* - z_c^*)$$
$$V_{ci}^* = (-\sin\kappa^* \cos\phi^*)(x_i^* - x_c^*) + (-\sin\kappa^* \sin\phi^* \sin\omega^* + \cos\kappa^* \cos\omega^*)(y_i^* - y_c^*)$$
$$+ (\sin\kappa^* \sin\phi^* \cos\omega^* + \cos\kappa^* \sin\omega^*)(z_i^* - z_c^*) \quad (2.12)$$
$$W_{ci}^* = (\sin\phi^*)(x_i^* - x_c^*) + (-\cos\phi^* \sin\omega^*)(y_i^* - y_c^*) + (\cos\phi^* \cos\omega^*)(z_i^* - z_c^*)$$

Applying the same collinearity principles from the previous section, we arrive at the same result as (2.9), except that now the image coordinates are a function of the tunnel coordinates, not the model coordinates. The result is

$$u_{ci} = u_c - f\frac{U_{ci}^*}{W_{ci}^*} = u_{ci}(\vec{q})$$
$$v_{ci} = v_c - f\frac{V_{ci}^*}{W_{ci}^*} = v_{ci}(\vec{q}) \quad (2.13)$$

The right side of Equation (2.13) shows that now the only unknown parameters remaining in u_{ci} and v_{ci} are the position and attitude parameters of the model. They have been grouped into the vector $\vec{q}$, given by

$$\vec{q}^T = [\Delta x, \Delta y, \Delta z, \alpha, \beta, \phi] \quad (2.14)$$

According to Dr. Ruyten, to solve for the six unknown position and attitude parameters, the minimization of a least squares sum is used. [7] That sum is called the χ^2 merit function, and it is the difference between the photographed image coordinates of the targets, denoted by $\tilde{u}_{ci}$ and $\tilde{v}_{ci}$, and the image coordinates as a function of the unknown parameters $\vec{q}$, given by

$$\chi^2(\vec{q}) = \sum_c \sum_i \{(u_{ci}(\vec{q}) - \tilde{u}_{ci})^2 + (v_{ci}(\vec{q}) - \tilde{v}_{ci})^2\} \quad (2.15)$$

The summation index c shows that this function is summed over all cameras, if there are more than one, and i indicates that it is summed over all target coordinates. Dr. Ruyten also explains that a function closely related to the χ^2 merit function is the rms fit error. "This error gives the rms deviation (in pixels) between measured and fitted image coordinates." [7] The rms fit error function is given by

$$\sigma(\vec{q}) = \left[\frac{1}{N}\chi^2(\vec{q})\right]^{\frac{1}{2}} \qquad (2.16)$$

where N is the total number of image coordinate pairs.

A successful minimization of the χ^2 merit function will result in values for each of the unknown position and attitude parameters. However, because there are six unknown parameters, minimizing this function is difficult. It requires a multi-parameter optimization scheme. The method employed is called a Levenberg-Marquardt algorithm, and is explained in the next section.

2.3 Levenberg-Marquardt

Levenberg-Marquardt is one of many non-linear methods of data modeling, or multi-parameter optimization. However, Dr. Ruyten has chosen to use the LM method because, as he says [7]

> Experience has shown that (even when employing as many as 94 fit parameters – six for model alignment and 11 parameters for 8 cameras each) satisfactory convergence of the LM algorithm is typically reached in 1-10 itereations. This constitutes a significant speed-up over the simplex method that was employed [before].

The book *Numerical Recipes in Fortran* [11] does an excellent job of explaining the LM algorithm. In general, LM follows these steps:

> (1) Pick initial values for the unknown parameters. Usually this will be 0, but in the case of the actual wind tunnel these could be the preliminary values read from the machine gages.

(2) Evaluate χ^2 using initial values and image data.

(3) Increment the unknown parameters by a small amount, and re-evaluate χ^2.

(4) If the new χ^2 is greater than the previous one, increase the increment by a factor of 10, and evaluate again.

(5) If the new χ^2 is less than the previous one, decrease the increment by a factor of 10, and evaluate again.

(6) Continue until the difference in the functions is less than some tolerance, typically 10^{-3}.

The first two steps are relatively easy, as are evaluating whether χ^2 has increased or decreased. The true heart of this nonlinear method is determining the magnitude and direction in which to increment the unknown parameters. Close to the minimum, the χ^2 function is expected to be well approximated by a quadratic form, which can be written as

$$\chi^2(\vec{q}) \approx \gamma - \mathbf{d} \cdot \vec{q} + \frac{1}{2}\vec{q} \cdot \mathbf{D} \cdot \vec{q} \qquad (2.17)$$

where $\mathbf{d}$ is an M-vector, and $\mathbf{D}$ is an $M \times M$ matrix. If this approximation is a good one, we can jump from the current trial parameters, $\vec{q}_{cur}$, to the minimizing ones, $\vec{q}_{min}$, in a single leap, given by

$$\vec{q}_{min} = \vec{q}_{cur} + \mathbf{D}^{-1} \cdot \left[-\nabla \chi^2(\vec{q}_{cur})\right] \qquad (2.18)$$

However, this may be a poor local approximation to the shape of the function that we are trying to minimize at $\vec{q}_{cur}$. If this is true, the best we can do is to step down the gradient using the steepest decent, given by

$$\vec{q}_{next} = \vec{q}_{cur} - constant \times \nabla \chi^2(\vec{q}_{cur}) \qquad (2.19)$$

where the constant is small enough not to exhaust the downhill direction.

To use Equations 2.18 and 2.19, we need to be able to compute the gradient of the χ^2 function at any set of parameters $\vec{q}$. To use Equation 2.18 we also need the matrix $\mathbf{D}$, which is the second derivative matrix (Hessian matrix) of the χ^2 merit function, at any $\vec{q}$.

We have specified the χ^2 merit function, therefore the Hessian matrix is known to us. Therefore, we can use Equation 2.18 whenever we choose to. The only reason to use Equation 2.19 will be if Equation 2.18 fails to improve the fit, signaling failure of Equation 2.17 as a good local approximation.

First, we need to determine partial derivatives of χ^2 with respect to the set of M unknown parameters in $\vec{q}$. Taking partial derivatives once arrives at the gradient (Equation 2.20), which will be zero at the χ^2 minimum.

$$\frac{\partial \chi^2}{\partial q_k} = -2 \sum_c \sum_i \left[(u_{ci}(\vec{q}) - \tilde{u}_{ci}) \frac{\partial u_{ci}(\vec{q})}{\partial q_k} + (v_{ci}(\vec{q}) - \tilde{v}_{ci}) \frac{\partial v_{ci}(\vec{q})}{\partial q_k} \right]$$

$$k = 1, 2, ..., M \qquad (2.20)$$

Taking an additional partial derivative yields Equation 2.21

$$\frac{\partial^2 \chi^2}{\partial q_k \partial q_l} = 2 \sum_c \sum_i \left[\frac{\partial u_{ci}(\vec{q})}{\partial q_k} \frac{\partial u_{ci}(\vec{q})}{\partial q_l} - \left[u_{ci}(\vec{q}) - \tilde{u}_{ci} \right] \frac{\partial^2 u_{ci}(\vec{q})}{\partial q_l \partial q_k} + \frac{\partial v_{ci}(\vec{q})}{\partial q_k} \frac{\partial v_{ci}(\vec{q})}{\partial q_l} - \left[v_{ci}(\vec{q}) - \tilde{v}_{ci} \right] \frac{\partial^2 v_{ci}(\vec{q})}{\partial q_l \partial q_k} \right] \qquad (2.21)$$

However, the $\frac{\partial^2}{\partial q_l \partial q_k}$ terms are deemed sufficiently small, and the equation reduces to

$$\frac{\partial^2 \chi^2}{\partial q_k \partial q_l} = 2 \sum_c \sum_i \left[\frac{\partial u_{ci}(\vec{q})}{\partial q_k} \frac{\partial u_{ci}(\vec{q})}{\partial q_l} + \frac{\partial v_{ci}(\vec{q})}{\partial q_k} \frac{\partial v_{ci}(\vec{q})}{\partial q_l} \right] \qquad (2.22)$$

We now need to solve for the partial derivatives of $u_{ci}(\vec{q})$ and $v_{ci}(\vec{q})$ with respect to each of the six unknown parameters. The partial derivatives are given as

$$\frac{\partial u_{ci}(\vec{q})}{\partial q_k} = -\frac{f}{W_{ci}}\left[(\cos\kappa^*\cos\phi^*)(\frac{\partial x_i^*}{\partial q_k}) + (\cos\kappa^*\sin\phi^*\sin\omega^* + \sin\kappa^*\cos\omega^*)(\frac{\partial y_i^*}{\partial q_k})\right.$$
$$\left. + (-\cos\kappa^*\sin\phi^*\cos\omega^* + \sin\kappa^*\sin\omega^*)(\frac{\partial z_i^*}{\partial q_k})\right]$$
$$+ \frac{fU_{ci}}{W_{ki}^2}\left[(\sin\phi^*)(\frac{\partial x_i^*}{\partial q_k}) + (-\cos\phi^*\sin\omega^*)(\frac{\partial y_i^*}{\partial q_k}) + (\cos\phi^*\cos\omega^*)(\frac{\partial z_i^*}{\partial q_k})\right]$$
(2.23)

$$\frac{\partial v_{ci}(\vec{q})}{\partial q_k} = -\frac{f}{W_{ci}}\left[(-\sin\kappa^*\cos\phi^*)(\frac{\partial x_i^*}{\partial q_k}) + (-\sin\kappa^*\sin\phi^*\sin\omega^* + \cos\kappa^*\cos\omega^*)(\frac{\partial y_i^*}{\partial q_k})\right.$$
$$\left. + (\sin\kappa^*\sin\phi^*\cos\omega^* + \cos\kappa^*\sin\omega^*)(\frac{\partial z_i^*}{\partial q_k})\right]$$
$$+ \frac{fV_{ci}}{W_{ki}^2}\left[(\sin\phi^*)(\frac{\partial x_i^*}{\partial q_k}) + (-\cos\phi^*\sin\omega^*)(\frac{\partial y_i^*}{\partial q_k}) + (\cos\phi^*\cos\omega^*)(\frac{\partial z_i^*}{\partial q_k})\right]$$

Notice in Equation 2.23 that only $\frac{\partial x_i^*}{\partial q_k}$, $\frac{\partial y_i^*}{\partial q_k}$, and $\frac{\partial z_i^*}{\partial q_k}$ change now as the unknown parameter, $\vec{q}$, with which the partial derivative is taken with respect to changes. These partial derivatives with respect to the six unknown position and attitude parameters are given as

$$\frac{\partial x_i^*}{\partial \Delta x} = 1$$
$$\frac{\partial x_i^*}{\partial \Delta y} = 0$$
$$\frac{\partial x_i^*}{\partial \Delta z} = 0$$
$$\frac{\partial x_i^*}{\partial \alpha} = \cos\beta(z_i^* - \Delta z)$$
$$\frac{\partial x_i^*}{\partial \beta} = (y_i^* - \Delta y)$$
(2.24)
$$\frac{\partial x_i^*}{\partial \phi} = y_i(-\sin\beta\sin\phi + \sin\alpha\cos\beta\cos\phi) -$$
$$(\sin\beta\cos\phi + \sin\alpha\cos\beta\sin\phi)z_i$$

$$\frac{\partial y_i^*}{\partial \Delta x} = 0$$

$$\frac{\partial y_i^*}{\partial \Delta y} = 1$$

$$\frac{\partial y_i^*}{\partial \Delta z} = 0$$

$$\frac{\partial y_i^*}{\partial \alpha} = -\sin\beta(z_i^* - \Delta z)$$

$$\frac{\partial y_i^*}{\partial \beta} = -(x_i^* - \Delta x) \qquad (2.25)$$

$$\frac{\partial y_i^*}{\partial \phi} = y_i(-\cos\beta\sin\phi - \sin\alpha\sin\beta\cos\phi) -$$

$$(\cos\beta\cos\phi - \sin\alpha\sin\beta\sin\phi)z_i$$

$$\frac{\partial z_i^*}{\partial \Delta x} = 0$$

$$\frac{\partial z_i^*}{\partial \Delta y} = 0$$

$$\frac{\partial z_i^*}{\partial \Delta z} = 1$$

$$\frac{\partial z_i^*}{\partial \alpha} = -\cos\beta(x_i^* - \Delta x) + \sin\beta(y_i^* - \Delta y)$$

$$\frac{\partial z_i^*}{\partial \beta} = 0 \qquad (2.26)$$

$$\frac{\partial z_i^*}{\partial \phi} = y_i(\cos\alpha\cos\phi) - (\cos\alpha\sin\phi)z_i$$

According to *Numerical Recipes* [11], it is conventional to remove the factors of 2 by defining

$$\beta_k = -\frac{1}{2}\frac{\partial \chi^2}{\partial q_k}$$

$$\alpha_{kl} = \frac{1}{2}\frac{\partial^2 \chi^2}{\partial q_k \partial q_l} \qquad (2.27)$$

making $[\alpha] = \frac{1}{2}\mathbf{D}$ in Equation (2.18), in terms of which that equation can be rewritten as the set of linear equations

$$\sum_{l=1}^{M} \alpha_{kl} \delta q_l = \beta_k \qquad (2.28)$$

This set is then solved for δq_l, which is the increment that is added to the unknown parameters. The key to the LM method is that it makes one big improvement over this standard method. Normally, δq_l equals some constant times β_l. However, Marquardt realized that the scale of this constant is dictated by the reciprocal of the diagonal element of the alpha matrix. He also inserted another factor, λ, which could be set to much less than one to reduce the step size. The result of these realizations is Equation (2.29).

$$\delta q_l = \frac{1}{\lambda \alpha_{ll}} \beta_l \qquad (2.29)$$

Marquardt also realized that Equation (2.29) could be combined with Equation (2.28) if a new matrix, α', is defined by

$$\alpha'_{jj} = \alpha_{jj}(1 + \lambda)$$
$$\alpha'_{jk} = \alpha_{jk} \qquad (2.30)$$

Which then yields Equation (2.31)

$$\sum_{l=1}^{M} \alpha'_{kl} \delta q_l = \beta_k \qquad (2.31)$$

This now is the set of linear equations the LM method uses to determine the increment to apply to the unknown parameters in $\vec{q}$.

The last step that remains in this process is to determine the precision of the fitted parameters. According to Dr. Ruyten, the precision of each fit parameter, q_k, is given by [7]

$$\sigma_{q_k} = \left[\frac{N}{2N - M}\right]^{\frac{1}{2}} \sigma(\vec{q}) C_{kk}^{\frac{1}{2}} \qquad (2.32)$$

where N is the number of image coordinate pairs, M is the number of fit parameters, $\sigma(\vec{q})$ is the rms fit error, given by Equation (2.16), and C_{kk} are the diagonal elements of the covariance matrix C. The covariance matrix C is found by inverting the curvature matrix, α_{kl}, given by Equation (2.27).

III. Deformation Modeling

Modeling of structural deformation can be an extremely complicated field, typically requiring some type of finite element analysis. We tried to compromise somewhere between a rigid model, which is what the current program uses, and a finite element analysis, which maybe too complicated to implement in a program such as this. Since the wings, horizontal, and vertical stabilizers of small scale aircraft test articles undergo significant deformation, we tailored our model for these structures. From his testing experience, Dr. Ruyten suggested that the deformation could be modeled by superposition of parabolic bending and linear twisting. [4]

3.1 Parabolic Bending

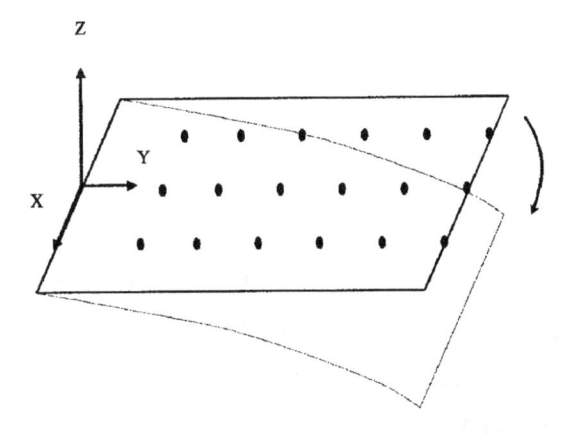

Figure 3.1   Parabolic Bending Set Up

Realistically, the wing would not bend linearly, such that the entire wing is deflected at a constant angle. It would be much more rigid near the fuselage where all of the structural support is, and would be more flexible near the tip due to the moment arm from the base of the wing to the tip. Thus, under severe aerodynamic loading,

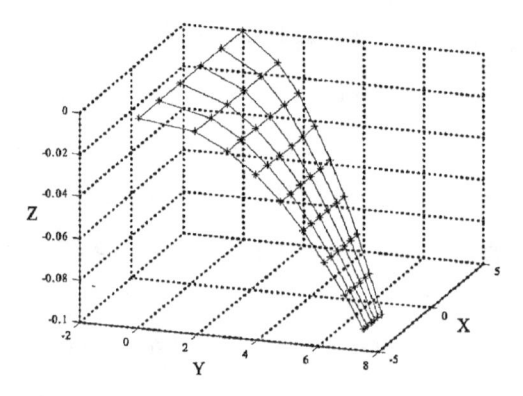

Figure 3.2   Wire-frame Bent Wing

the wing should deflect in a curved manner. This behavior can be approximated as parabolic bending. Figure 3.1 shows the deflection for parabolic bending.

The equation used to model parabolic bending is

$$z = K_{bend}\left(\frac{y}{L}\right)^2 \qquad (3.1)$$

where z is the deflection value, K_{bend} is the bending coefficient, y is the distance from the base of the wing to the target point, and L is the total length of the wing. Figure 3.2 shows a MATLAB-generated wire-frame model of a wing displaying parabolic bending. As will be discussed in the next chapter, the wing is the approximate dimensions of a Lockheed Martin F-22A Raptor wing, with a wing length of 6.78 meters. The bending coefficient is .1, meaning that the tip of the wing is .1m lower than an undeformed wing as shown in the figure.

There is a problem with simply applying the bend and twist equations to the undeformed coordinates to get deformed coordinates. The new Z value is calculated based on the bend and twist functions and the wing is essentially "stretched". For example a point that was on the wing tip, with a Y value of 6.78, would have a new Z value of, say, -.5, but would still have a Y value of 6.78. The wing is being elongated, and this is not a very accurate representation.

One way to account for this is to first calculate the path length from the origin to the undeformed point. Then, follow the curve of the bending function until it reaches that same path length. Find the new Y value for that path length and replace the old Y with the new one. In this way, the function no longer stretches the wing and is more accurate. To apply this to our bending function, we use a method prescribed in *Advanced Engineering Mathematics* [3]. We first find a parametric representation of the bend function, which is given by

$$\mathbf{r}(t) = t\hat{i} + \frac{BCt^2}{Y_{max}^2}\hat{j} \qquad (3.2)$$

Now, find the derivative with respect to the parameter t, which is given by

$$\mathbf{r}'(t) = t\hat{i} + \frac{2BCt}{Y_{max}^2}\hat{j} \qquad (3.3)$$

We now find $\mathbf{r}' \cdot \mathbf{r}'$, which is given by

$$\mathbf{r}' \cdot \mathbf{r}' = 1 + t\left[\frac{2BC}{Y_{max}^2}\right]^2 \qquad (3.4)$$

We can now apply this to the general equation for the arc length of a curve, which is given by

$$l = \int_a^b \sqrt{\mathbf{r}' \cdot \mathbf{r}'}\,dt \qquad (3.5)$$

where, in our case $a = 0$ and $b = Y$. For each point, we simply set l equal to the undeformed path length, and solve for the new Y value, which is the upper limit of integration. The undeformed path length is simply

$$l_{und} = \sqrt{X^2 + Y^2} \qquad (3.6)$$

This method of correction is not applied to the twisting function for two reasons. First, the twisting displacement is generally smaller than the bending displacement. Second, bending is only a function of one variable, and the path length will only vary in one direction. Thus it is correctable. Twisting is a function of X and Y, and therefore the parameterization of the path length is significantly more complex.

3.2 Linear Twist

The other mode of deformation being modeled is linear twisting. For this model we assume the base at the wing is rigidly attached to the fuselage and that the deflection is linear at each chord line, meaning that the positive deflection on the leading edge is equal in magnitude to the negative deflection on the trailing edge. However, at each increasing chord interval, that angle is increased. Thus the twist gets more and more severe. Figure 3.3 shows the set-up for linear twist.

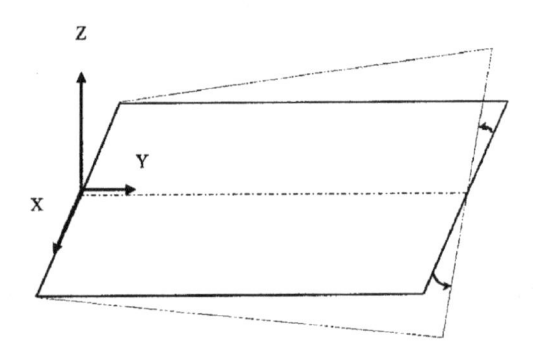

Figure 3.3   Linear Twisting Set Up

The general equation for linear twisting is

$$z = K_{twist}\left(\frac{y}{L}\right)\left(\frac{x}{X_{max}}\right) \qquad (3.7)$$

where z is the deflection value, K_{twist} is the twisting coefficient, y is the distance from the base of the wing to the target point, L is the total length of the wing, x is distance along the chord, from the origin to the target point, and X_{max} is the total chord length, at that particular target point. This function will provide no twist at the base, where y is equal to zero. It will also provide maximum twisting upwards at the tip on the leading edge, and maximum twisting downward on the trailing edge.

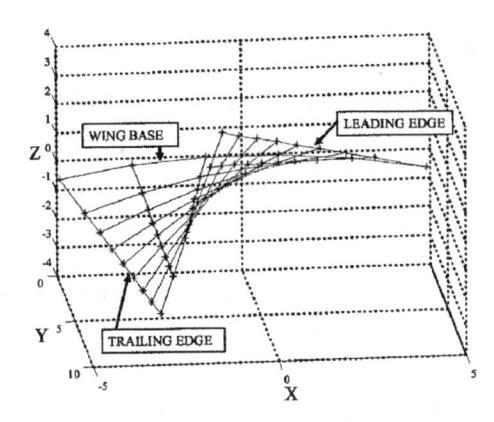

Figure 3.4   Wire-Frame Twisted Wing

Figure 3.4 shows a MATLAB-generated wire-frame model of a wing displaying linear twisting. This graph is a little deceptive, as it appears to have some curve to it. One difference is that the set up shows a rectangular wing, where as Figure 3.4 is again the F-22 modeled wing. The midline of the wing goes from the midpoint of the base to the midpoint of the tip, exactly dividing the wing in half at each chord interval. The twist is about this line, which is at an angle, compared to the rectangular wing which has it's midline perfectly straight. The other factor to account for is that this is a severely twisted wing (twist coefficient of 4), to show the effects of twisting. As previously mentioned, there is no way to correct for the stretching of the wing where twisting is concerned. Because of this, some stretching of the wing is evident in the graph. Thus, while the graph seems to show some curvature, it is in fact linear twisting. Hence, the equation for the total deflection, accounting for both parabolic bending and linear twist is

$$z = K_{bend}\left(\frac{y}{L}\right)^2 + K_{twist}\left(\frac{y}{L}\right)\left(\frac{x}{X_{max}}\right) \qquad (3.8)$$

3.3 Implementaion of Deformation Models

With equations for both the bending and twisting of the wing, we now need to integrate these into the Levenberg-Marquardt optimizer. Initially there were six unknown parameters, three for position and three for attitude. Now we will introduce two more unknown parameters, the bending and twisting coefficients. When the program tries to match position and attitude parameters to the given images, it understands there exists the possibility the images were taken from a deformed article. Solving for these deformation parameters will yield a more accurate solution for the position and attitude.

As stated in the previous chapter, the Levenberg-Marquardt method uses partial derivatives of the equations with respect to the unknown parameters to determine the step size and direction. Since we have included two new unknown parameters to solve for, this means calculating two new sets of partial derivatives.

Recall from Equation (2.23) that only $\frac{\partial x_i^*}{\partial q_k}$, $\frac{\partial y_i^*}{\partial q_k}$, and $\frac{\partial z_i^*}{\partial q_k}$ change as the unknown parameter with which the partial derivative is taken with respect to changes. Essentially, this means that to add in K_{bend} and K_{twist} as parameters, all that really needs to be solved are the partial derivatives of x_i^*, y_i^*, and z_i^* with respect to the unknown parameters, now including K_{bend}, and K_{twist}. Of course, x_i^*, y_i^*, and z_i^* now include the deformation functions.

First, we need to combine the equations governing deformation into the equations that transform target coordinates from the model frame to the image frame.

That is,

$$x_i^* = \Delta x + x_i(\cos\alpha\cos\beta) + y_i(\sin\beta\cos\phi + \sin\alpha\cos\beta\sin\phi)$$
$$+ \left[K_{twist}(\tfrac{y}{L})(\tfrac{x}{X_{max}}) - K_{bend}(\tfrac{y}{L})^2\right](-\sin\beta\sin\phi + \sin\alpha\cos\beta\cos\phi)$$

$$y_i^* = \Delta y + x_i(-\cos\alpha\sin\beta) + y_i(\cos\beta\cos\phi - \sin\alpha\sin\beta\sin\phi) \qquad (3.9)$$
$$+ \left[K_{twist}(\tfrac{y}{L})(\tfrac{x}{X_{max}}) - K_{bend}(\tfrac{y}{L})^2\right](-\cos\beta\sin\phi - \sin\alpha\sin\beta\cos\phi)$$

$$z_i^* = \Delta z + x_i(-\sin\alpha) + y_i(\cos\alpha\sin\phi) + \left[K_{twist}(\tfrac{y}{L})(\tfrac{x}{X_{max}}) - K_{bend}(\tfrac{y}{L})^2\right](\cos\alpha\cos\phi)$$

Now, simply take the partial derivatives of each with respect to all the unknown parameters, including K_{bend} and K_{twist}. This is given by

$$\frac{\partial x_i^*}{\partial \Delta x} = 1$$
$$\frac{\partial x_i^*}{\partial \Delta y} = 0$$
$$\frac{\partial x_i^*}{\partial \Delta z} = 0$$
$$\frac{\partial x_i^*}{\partial \alpha} = \cos\beta(z_i^* - \Delta z)$$
$$\frac{\partial x_i^*}{\partial \beta} = (y_i^* - \Delta y) \qquad (3.10)$$
$$\frac{\partial x_i^*}{\partial \phi} = y_i(-\sin\beta\sin\phi + \sin\alpha\cos\beta\cos\phi) -$$
$$(\sin\beta\cos\phi + \sin\alpha\cos\beta\sin\phi)\left[K_{twist}(\tfrac{y}{L})(\tfrac{x}{X_{max}}) - K_{bend}(\tfrac{y}{L})^2\right]$$
$$\frac{\partial x_i^*}{\partial K_{bend}} = -(-\sin\beta\sin\phi + \sin\alpha\cos\beta\cos\phi)(\tfrac{y}{L})^2$$
$$\frac{\partial x_i^*}{\partial K_{twist}} = (-\sin\beta\sin\phi + \sin\alpha\cos\beta\cos\phi)(\tfrac{y}{L})(\tfrac{x}{X_{max}})$$

$$\frac{\partial y_i^*}{\partial \Delta x} = 0$$

$$\frac{\partial y_i^*}{\partial \Delta y} = 1$$

$$\frac{\partial y_i^*}{\partial \Delta z} = 0$$

$$\frac{\partial y_i^*}{\partial \alpha} = -\sin\beta(z_i^* - \Delta z)$$

$$\frac{\partial y_i^*}{\partial \beta} = -(x_i^* - \Delta x) \qquad (3.11)$$

$$\frac{\partial y_i^*}{\partial \phi} = y_i(-\cos\beta\sin\phi - \sin\alpha\sin\beta\cos\phi) -$$
$$(\cos\beta\cos\phi - \sin\alpha\sin\beta\sin\phi)\left[K_{twist}(\tfrac{y}{L})(\tfrac{x}{X_{max}}) - K_{bend}(\tfrac{y}{L})^2\right]$$

$$\frac{\partial y_i^*}{\partial K_{bend}} = -(-\cos\beta\sin\phi - \sin\alpha\sin\beta\cos\phi)(\tfrac{y}{L})^2$$

$$\frac{\partial y_i^*}{\partial K_{twist}} = (-\cos\beta\sin\phi - \sin\alpha\sin\beta\cos\phi)(\tfrac{y}{L})(\tfrac{x}{X_{max}})$$

$$\frac{\partial z_i^*}{\partial \Delta x} = 0$$

$$\frac{\partial z_i^*}{\partial \Delta y} = 0$$

$$\frac{\partial z_i^*}{\partial \Delta z} = 1$$

$$\frac{\partial z_i^*}{\partial \alpha} = -\cos\beta(x_i^* - \Delta x) + \sin\beta(y_i^* - \Delta y)$$

$$\frac{\partial z_i^*}{\partial \beta} = 0 \qquad (3.12)$$

$$\frac{\partial z_i^*}{\partial \phi} = y_i(\cos\alpha\cos\phi) - (\cos\alpha\sin\phi)\left[K_{twist}(\tfrac{y}{L})(\tfrac{x}{X_{max}}) - K_{bend}(\tfrac{y}{L})^2\right]$$

$$\frac{\partial z_i^*}{\partial K_{bend}} = -(\cos\alpha\cos\phi)(\tfrac{y}{L})^2$$

$$\frac{\partial z_i^*}{\partial K_{twist}} = (\cos\alpha\cos\phi)(\tfrac{y}{L})(\tfrac{x}{X_{max}})$$

The equations which convert the coordinates of the targets from the model frame into pixel coordinates in the image frame were modified to include the deformation functions prescribed. Partial derivatives of those functions were taken with respect to the old unknown position and attitude parameters, as well as the new coefficients and bending and twisting. These partial differential equations can now be coded into SUBROUTINE mrqfun1 of the Fortran code (see Appendix B). The program is now modified and ready to account for deformation of the test article.

3.4 Evaluating the Deformation Model

Now needed is some way to evaluate the model with deformation against the original rigid body program to determine how much of an improvement has been made. To aid in the evaluation, a program was written in MATLAB to construct a hypothetical test article to be used as the "truth model". By comparing the original and modified programs to this truth model, quantitative error improvement results can be obtained. The code for this MATLAB program is shown in Appendix A.

The test article in the truth model is based on the approximate dimensions of a Lockheed Martin F-22A Raptor. The test article includes a rigid fuselage which is 19 meters long and 4 meters wide, and a wing that is 6.78 meters from base to tip, 9.85 meters long along the base, and 1.66 meters long along the tip. The wing can bend according to the parabolic bending and linear twisting defined in the previous chapter. This set up is shown in Figure 3.5.

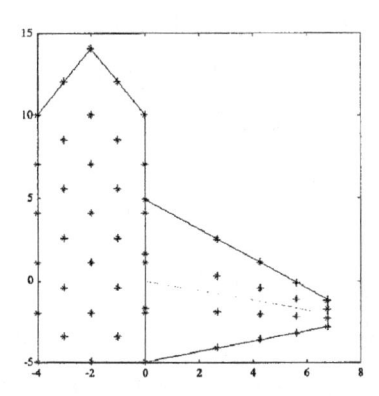

Figure 3.5   Set-up of Truth Model Test Article

3.4.1 Target Distribution.

One of the features of the truth model program is the ability to easily change the number and density of target locations on the wing. This helps answer the question of how many targets is optimal, and what kind of spacing is desired.

The program uses three variables, X Density Factor (XDF), Y Density Factor (YDF), and Y Cluster Factor (YCF), to set the number and spacing of the targets. The density factor divides the wing into that number of sections, with a target on the wing edge and targets between sections. Thus, with an XDF of 3 and a YDF of 4, you will get a total of 20 targets on the wing. In the x-direction, we space the targets equally using the interval

$$m = \frac{X_{max} - X_{min}}{XDF} \qquad (3.13)$$

So, an XDF of 3 divides the wing, in the X direction, into 3 sections of the same size, meaning that at each Y interval there will be 4 targets, 2 on the edges and 2 in between.

In the y-direction, a grid of equally spaced targets on the wing is not desired because the majority of the deformation will be occurring near the wing tip. The desired grid is one more densely populated near the wing tip. Thus, the YCF variable is introduced. YCF determines by what order the spacing between Y intervals decreases. For example, a YCF of 2 indicates that the spacing between each interval will decrease parabolically.

Figure 3.6 shows the set up to determine the Y interval. We first define a curve given by Y^{YCF}, where the endpoint is the wingspan, L, which gives a function value of Y_{max}^{YCF}. This ensures that the Y intervals end on the wing tip. To determine the Y spacing, the interval size is first determined by

$$n = \frac{(L)^{YCF}}{YDF} \qquad (3.14)$$

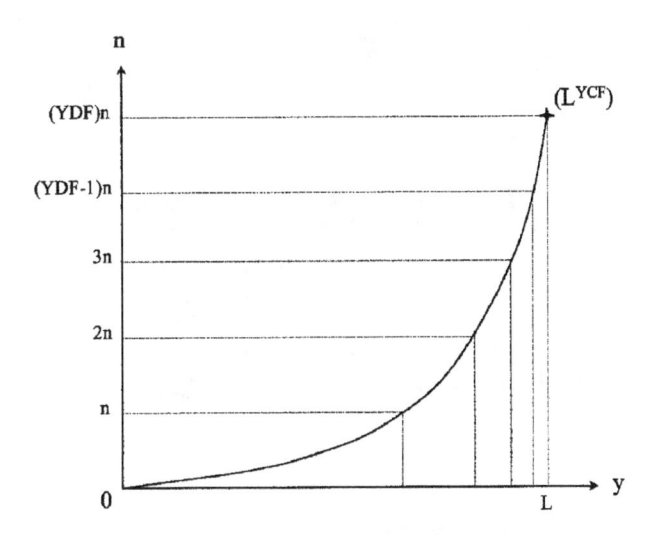

Figure 3.6   Set-Up of Y Interval Determination

Then, at each interval $N = n, 2n, 3n, ..., (YDF-1)n, (YDF)n$, the Y value is determined by

$$Y = N^{\frac{1}{YCF}} \tag{3.15}$$

3.4.2 Camera Views.   After all the coordinates of the test article have been calculated, the program will then show the perspective of each of eight cameras, and how the test article will look to that camera. This gives the user a nice sense of how much the test article has been deformed.

The program can show anywhere from one to eight camera views. Cameras are placed at 45 degree intervals, all in a plane that is approximately in the center (midway from tail to nose) of the fuselage. The camera set up is seen in Figure 3.7, which is looking down the wind tunnel at the test aritcle head on. Sample camera views in pixel coordinates are shown in Figures 3.8 and 3.9. This sample has the test article at $\alpha = 0$, $\beta = 0$, $\phi = 0$, a bending coefficient of .7, and a twisting coefficient of .1. This makes for a fairly deformed wing, as cameras 3 and 7 show. In

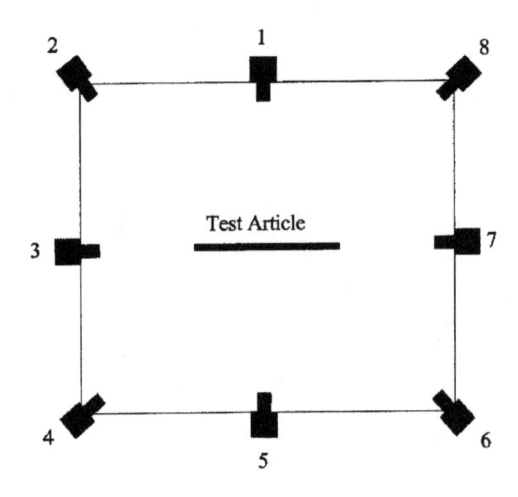

Figure 3.7   Wind Tunnel Camera Set Up

an undeformed case, cameras 3 and 7 would only show a straight line because they are stationed directly off the wingtips.

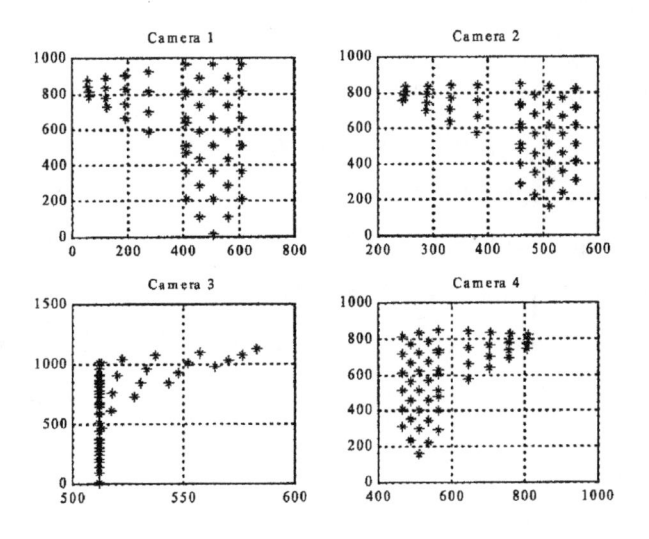

Figure 3.8   Sample View of Cameras 1-4

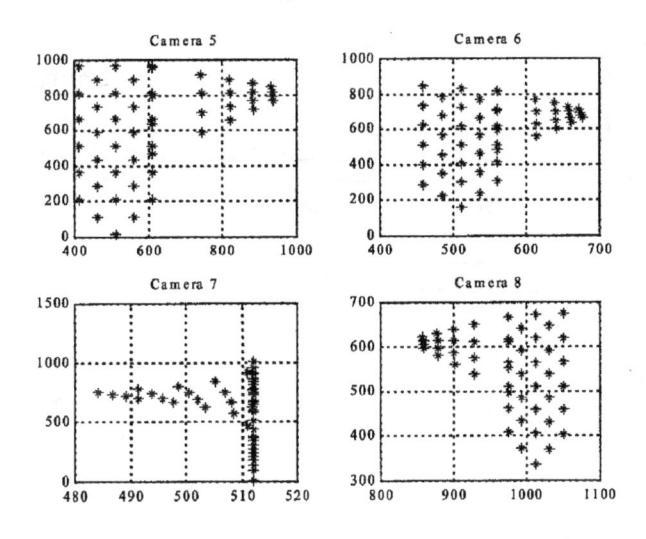

Figure 3.9   Sample View of Cameras 5-8

IV. Results

An analysis is performed to determine how the error in position and attitude varies as the number of targets, YCF, and number and location of cameras are changed. The aim is to optimize these parameters so that we may better evaluate the performance of the new bending model versus the old rigid model. Many runs of each program were accomplished to make these charts, and the raw data for each run can be found in Appendix C. In all test cases, the test article was set at the following position and attitude: $\Delta x = 5$ m, $\Delta y = 0$ m, $\Delta z = -20$ m, $\alpha = 15$ deg, $\beta = 10$ deg, and $\phi = 5$ deg.

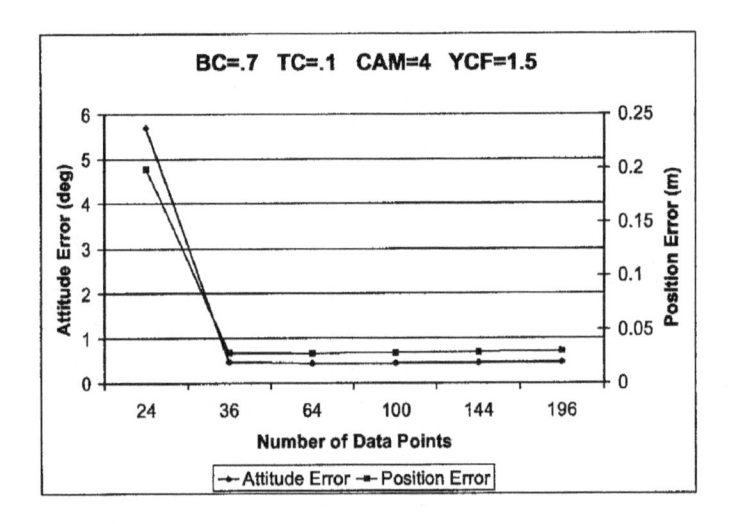

Figure 4.1   Relative Error Versus Number of Data Points, Severely Deformed

Figures 4.1 and 4.2 show the results of the target number study, computed using 4 cameras. As seen in the graphs, after a certain number of data points the relative error of position and attitude due to number of targets is fairly constant. This study was performed on both a severely deformed wing (BC=.7 TC=.1) and

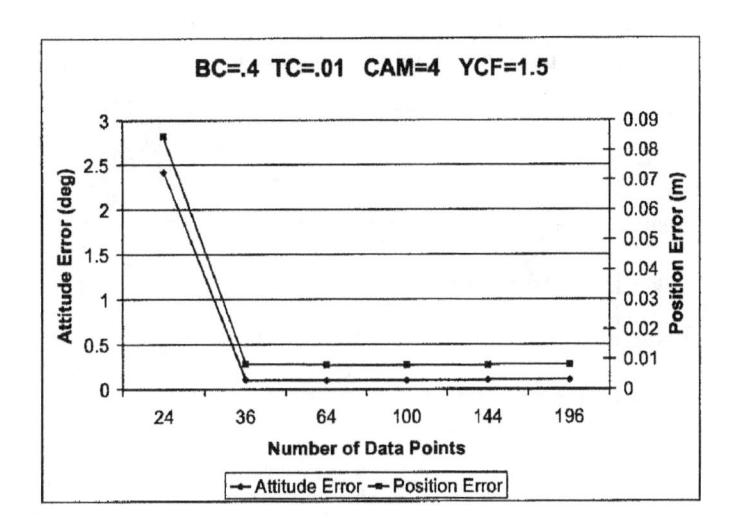

Figure 4.2   Relative Error Versus Number of Data Points, Moderately Deformed

a moderately deformed one (BC=.4 TC=.01) to ensure consistency. Fifty targets was deemed to be sufficiently into this regime. Bear in mind that 50 is the number of data points, not necessarily the number of targets on the test article. Thus, in a 4-camera configuration, the actual number of targets is about 13.

Figure 4.3 shows the results of the Y cluster factor study. The Y density factor was bumped up to 8 to give more divisions in the Y axis. This was done to capture the spectrum from evenly spaced to tightly packed towards the wing tip. The graph shows a pretty even trend that error gets worse as the points are packed tighter and tighter towards the wing tip. It also shows a drop in error around YCF=1.25, which is not quite evenly spaced, but still provides good coverage of the whole wing. Figure 4.4 shows the difference in the target layouts of YCF=1 and YCF=1.25.

Figures 4.5 and 4.6 show the results of the camera study, one with moderate bending and one with more severe bending. This graph uses the same camera set up as in Figure 3.7. In the graph, 4 denotes cameras 1-4, and 8 denotes all 8 cameras.

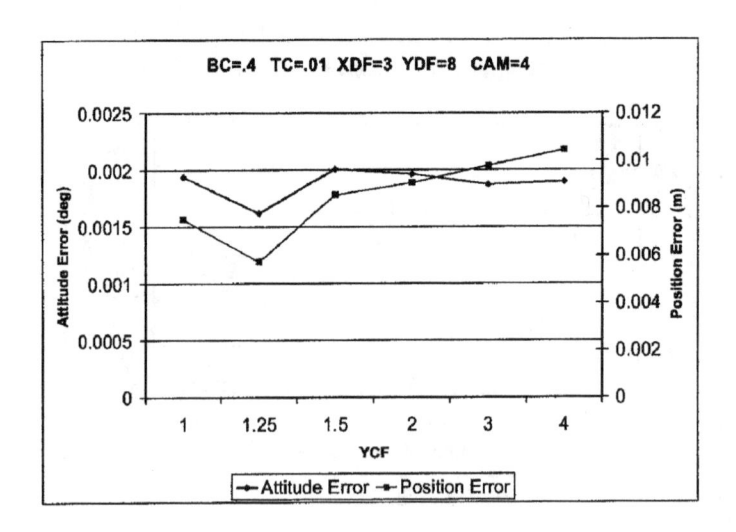

Figure 4.3   Relative Error Versus YCF

A surprising result is that more cameras does not necessarily seem to be better. In fact, 2 cameras offset by 90 degrees performs as well as, if not better than, 4 or 8 cameras.

We now have optimum camera and target conditions, and can evaluate the two position and attitude models; the old rigid model, and the new model which includes bending and twisting. Figure 4.7 shows the results of the bending study. As seen in the graph, and as is expected, as the bending coefficient gets more and more severe, the new bending model outperforms the old rigid model by greater margins. The same can be said for the performance in the presence of twist, shown in Figure 4.8.

One last area to evaluate is how each model performs in the presence of noise. Neither method is going to have perfect measurements, and thus noise will affect each. Figure 4.9 shows the effects of increasing noise on each model. At low levels of noise, the margin between the rigid model and the bend/twist model remains fairly constant. In extremely noisy conditions, behavior begins to diminish.

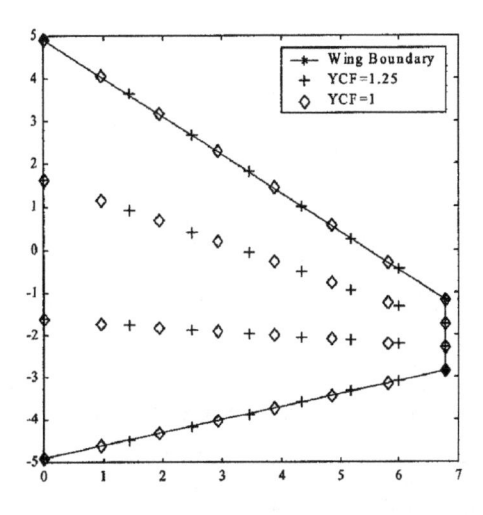

Figure 4.4   Comparison of YCF=1 to YCF=1.25

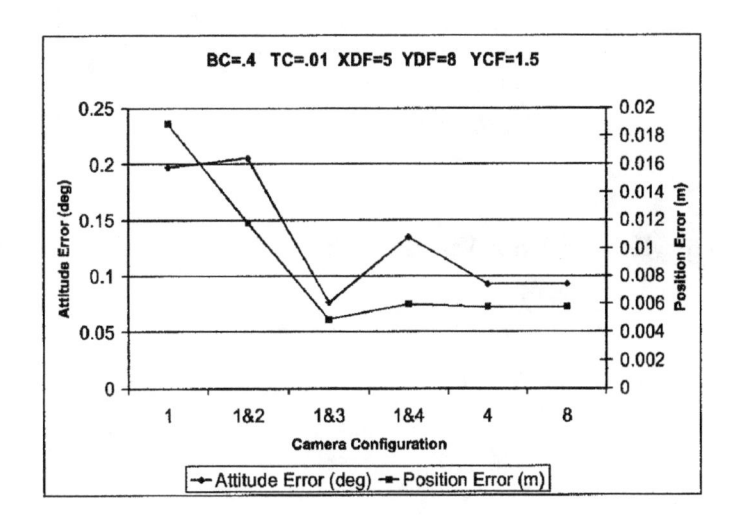

Figure 4.5   Relative error versus number of cameras, moderate bending

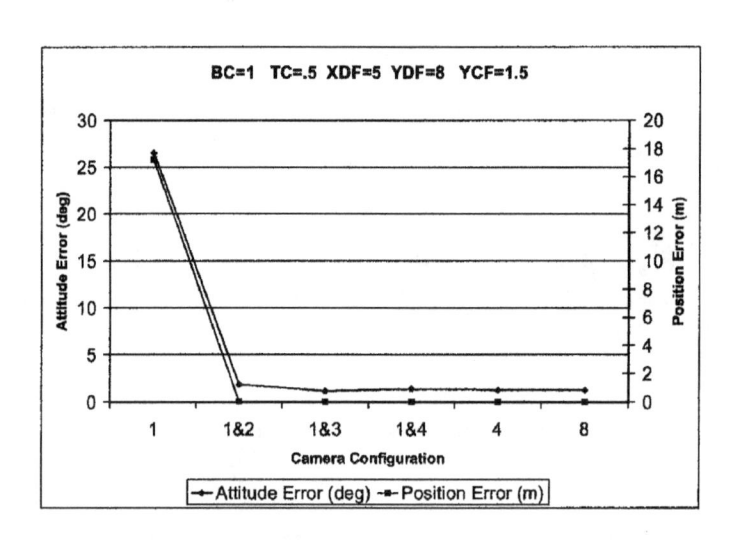

Figure 4.6   Relative Error Versus Number of Cameras, Severe bending

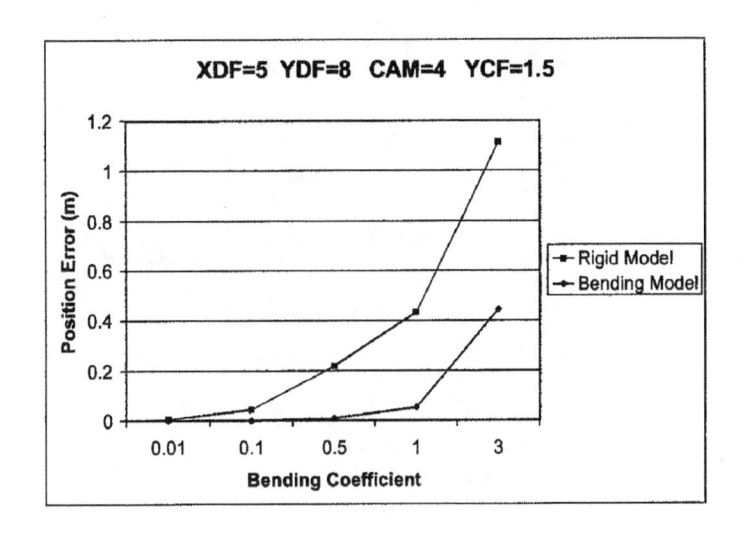

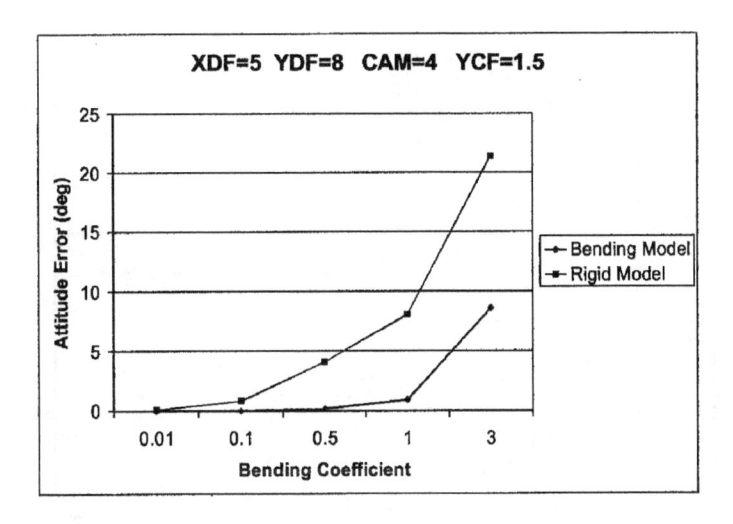

Figure 4.7   Relative Error Versus Bending Coefficient for Bending and Rigid Models

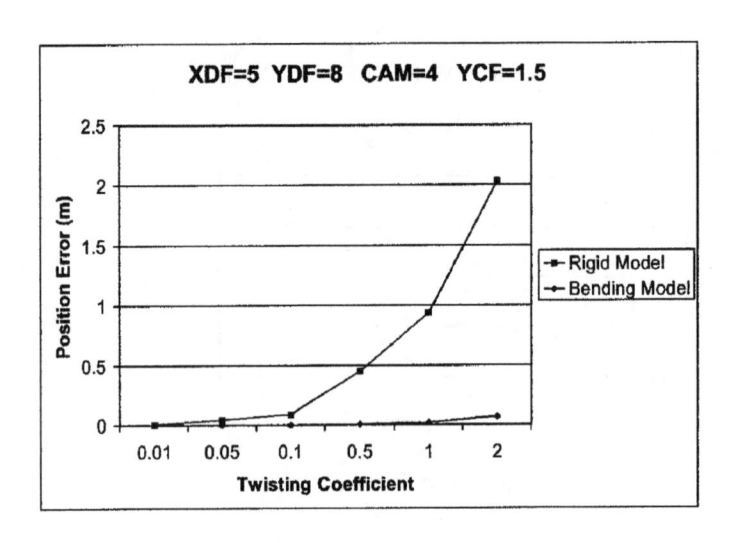

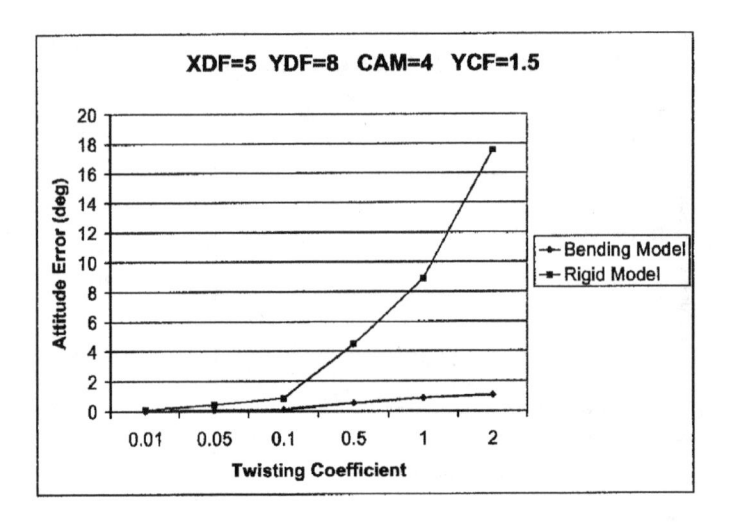

Figure 4.8   Relative Error Versus Twisting Coefficient for Bending and Rigid Models

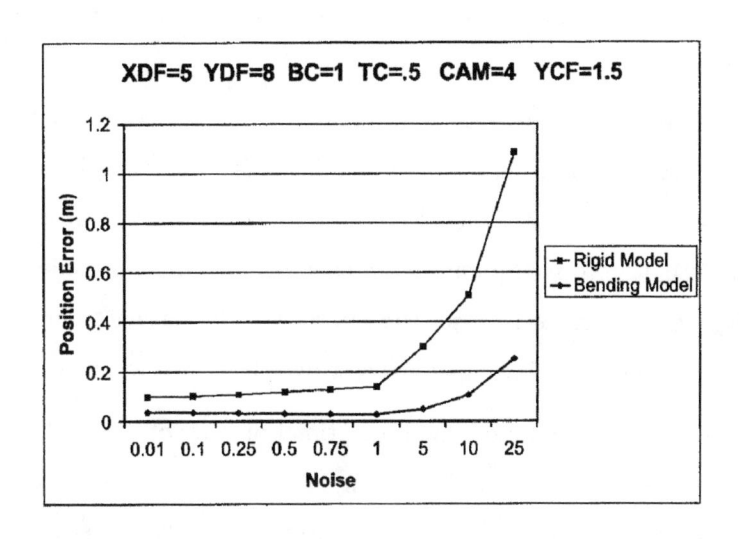

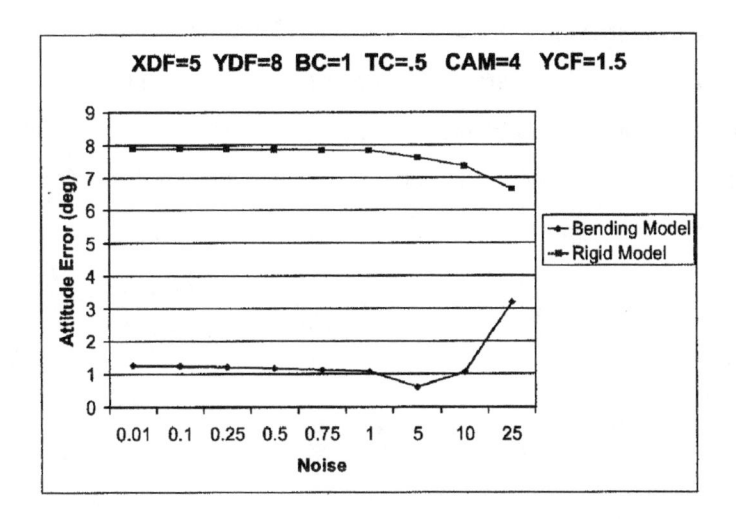

Figure 4.9 Relative Error Versus Noise Level for Bending and Rigid Models

V. Conclusions

The main objective of this thesis was to improve AEDC's current method of position and attitude determination to account for deformation of the test article. The results showed that by adding in bending and twisting coefficients, dramatic increases in accuracy of position and attitude determination could be achieved for simulated data with a simple deformation model. The next step to continue the work of this thesis would be to incorporate more complex deformation models, possibly using a finite element analysis. Also, the improved deformation model should be compared against the original using actual test data from real wind tunnel models.

This thesis was also to determine the optimal number of targets and cameras to achieve the greatest accuracy, while staying in reasonable numbers. It was found that at least 50 targets are required to achieve optimal accuracy, while any more than that did not add a whole lot of benefit. A YCF of 1.25 was found to provide the best accuracy. This was more clustered than a straight linear distribution, but not quite as dense at the wing tip as a parabolic distribution. It was expected from previous data runs that 4 cameras would provide the optimal solution, but when actually graphed out, 2 cameras spaced at 90 degrees provided slightly better results.

Appendix A. MATLAB Code

```
%%%%%%%%%%%%%%%%%%%%%%%%%%%%%%%%%
% Thesis: F-22 Wing Target Assignment  %
% Author: 1Lt Sean A. Krolikowski       %
% Date: 31 August 2000                  %
%%%%%%%%%%%%%%%%%%%%%%%%%%%%%%%%%

clear all
%Establish wing and fuselage boundaries from specs
Xr=[-4.925 4.925 -1.185 -2.852 -4.925]; Yr=[0 0 6.78 6.78 0];
Yf=[2 -2 -2 0 2 2]; Xf=[0 0 15 19 15 0]; Yf=Yf-2; Xf=Xf-4.925;

figure(1),clf plot(Yr,Xr,'*-'),axis square,hold on
plot(Yf,Xf,'*-')


%Set the Density Factors: XDF and YDF
%This will specify how dense the grid points are
%in the X and Y directions
XDF=5; YDF=7;


%Set the Y Cluster Factor, YCF
%This will specify how clustered the grid points are
%towards the wing tip
%   NOTE: If for some reason the wing is reconfigured to allow
%   a negative y value, you should not enter an odd number for the YCF
YCF=1.25;

%Compute Grid Points
Ymin=0; Ymax=6.78; w=Ymin; t=1; i=0; n=((Ymax-Ymin)^YCF)/YDF; N=n;
while w <= Ymax
   Xmin=.30557522*w-4.925;
   Xmax=-.9*w+4.925;
   Xmid=(Xmax+Xmin)/2;
    q=Xmin;
   index=1;
   m=(Xmax-Xmin)/XDF;
   for index=1:(XDF+1)
      X(t,1)=q;
      Xbar(t,1)=Xmid;
      XM(t,1)=Xmax;
      Y(t,1)=w;
    t=t+1;
```

```
        q=q+m;
        index=index+1;
    end
    w=N^(1/YCF);
    N=N+n;
    i=i+1;
end

%Establish Fuselage Targets
YF=[-2 0 2 -1 1 -2 0 2 -1 1 -2 0 2 -1 1 -2 0 2 -1 1 -2 0 2 -1 1 -2
0 2 -1 1 0]; XF=[0 0 0 1.5 1.5 3 3 3 4.5 4.5 6 6 6 7.5 7.5 9 9 9
10.5 10.5 12 12 12 13.5 13.5 15 15 15 17 17 19]; YF=YF-2;
XF=XF-4.925; Flength=length(XF);

%Draw Grid
plot(Y,X,'*r'),plot(YF,XF,'*r'),plot(Y,Xbar,'g'),hold off

%Set Bending and Twisting Coefficients
BC=1; TC=.5;

%Determine Undeformed Path Lengths
length=length(X); l=1; for l=1:length
    L(l,1)=(X(l,1)^2+Y(l,1)^2)^.5;
    l=l+1;
end

%Calcualte Twist Angle
TA=atan(Xbar(length,1)/Y(length,1));

%Solve for corrected Y coords, given path length
a=(2*BC/Ymax^2)^2;


for j=1:length tlen=Y(j,1); told=0; tnew=7; if BC==0
    Ynew(j,1)=Y(j,1);
    Z(j,1)=0;
else
    while abs(tnew-told)>1e-12
    told=tnew;
    tnew=told-(1/2*told*(a*told^2+1)^(1/2)+1/2/a^(1/2)*1*log(a^(1/2)*told+(a*told^2+1)^(1/2))-tlen)/...
        ((a^2*told^3+a*told+a^(3/2)*told^2*(a*told^2+1)^(1/2)+a^(1/2)*(a*told^2+1)^(1/2))/a^(1/2)/...
        (a*told^2+1)^(1/2)/(a^(1/2)*told+(a*told^2+1)^(1/2)));
    end
```

```
        Ynew(j,1)=tnew;
        XT(j,1)=X(j,1)*cos(TA)-Y(j,1)*sin(TA);
        XTM(j,1)=XM(j,1)*cos(TA)-Y(j,1)*sin(TA);
        YT(j,1)=X(j,1)*sin(TA)+Ynew(j,1)*cos(TA);
        Z(j,1)=-BC*(tnew/Ymax)^2+TC*(YT(j,1)/Ymax)*(XT(j,1)/XTM(j,1));
end end

%Set Up for 3D Grid
figure(2),clf for j=0:i-1
    plot3(Ynew(j*XDF+j+1:(j+1)*XDF+j+1,1),X(j*XDF+j+1:(j+1)*XDF+j+1,1),Z(j*XDF+j+1:(j+1)*XDF+j+1,1),'*-'),hold on
end

s=1; for k=1:XDF+1
    for l=0:i-1
        YY(s,1)=Ynew(k+l*(XDF+1));
        XX(s,1)=X(k+l*(XDF+1));
        ZZ(s,1)=Z(k+l*(XDF+1));
        s=s+1;
    end
end

for j=0:XDF
    plot3(YY(j*i+1:(j+1)*i,1),XX(j*i+1:(j+1)*i,1),ZZ(j*i+1:(j+1)*i,1),'*-')
end hold off

%Convert target coords from wing frame to model frame
DX=4.925; DY=2; for j=1:length
    Xi(j,1)=X(j,1)+DX;
    Yi(j,1)=Ynew(j,1)+DY;
    Yunbent(j,1)=Y(j,1)+DY;
    Zi(j,1)=Z(j,1);
    Zunbent(j,1)=0;
end XF=XF+DX; YF=YF+DY;

%Add fuselage points to data set
%for j=1:Flength
%    Xi(length+j,1)=XF(1,j);
%    Yi(length+j,1)=YF(1,j);
%    Yunbent(length+j,1)=YF(1,j);
%    Zi(length+j,1)=0;
%    Zunbent(length+j,1)=0;
%end
%length=max(size(Xi));
```

A-3

```
%Print Model Coords to file for FORTRAN
data = [transpose(Xi);transpose(Yi);transpose(Zi)]; data2 =
[transpose(Xi);transpose(Yunbent);transpose(Zunbent)]; fid =
fopen('data.in','w');
fprintf(fid,'%5.0f\n',length);
fprintf(fid,'%5.5f\n',BC);
fprintf(fid,'%5.5f\n',TC);
fprintf(fid,'%5.5f\n',DX);
fprintf(fid,'%5.5f\n',DY);
fprintf(fid,'%5.5f\n',Ymax);
fprintf(fid,'%4.10f    %4.10f    %4.10f\n',data);
fprintf(fid,'%4.10f    %4.10f    %4.10f\n',data2);
fclose(fid);

%Set Model Orientation, alpha is pitch, beta is yaw, and phi is roll
alpha=0; beta=0; phi=0;

%Convert angles to radians and evaluate sin and cos
alpha=alpha*(pi/180); beta=beta*(pi/180); phi=phi*(pi/180);
ca=cos(alpha); sa=sin(alpha); cb=cos(beta); sb=sin(beta);
cp=cos(phi); sp=sin(phi);

%Set displacement of model frame origin from TRS
delxk=5; delyk=0; delzk=-20;

%Convert target coords from model frame to TRS
for j=1:length
    Xistar(j,1)=delxk+Xi(j,1)*ca*cb+Yi(j,1)*(sb*cp+sa*cb*sp)+Zi(j,1)*(-sb*sp+sa*cb*cp);
    Yistar(j,1)=delyk+Xi(j,1)*-ca*sb+Yi(j,1)*(cb*cp-sa*sb*sp)+Zi(j,1)*(-cb*sp-sa*sb*cp);
    Zistar(j,1)=delzk+Xi(j,1)*-sa+Yi(j,1)*ca*sp+Zi(j,1)*ca*cp;
end

%Set camera parameters:
%uc and vc are the location of the camera focus in the camera frame, should be the same for each camera
%f is the focal length, also should be the same
%Assume the camera uses a resolution of 1024x1024, with the origin at the bottom right corner
uc=512; vc=512; f=1000;

%Define postion and attitude of Camera 1
xc1=14; yc1=0; zc1=-40; phic1=0; kappac1=0; omegac1=0;
phic1=phic1*(pi/180); kappac1=kappac1*(pi/180);
omegac1=omegac1*(pi/180); cp1=cos(phic1); sp1=sin(phic1);
```

```
ck1=cos(kappac1); sk1=sin(kappac1); co1=cos(omegac1);
so1=sin(omegac1);

%Find target coords in camera frame
for j=1:length
    Uci1(j,1)=(Xistar(j,1)-xc1)*cp1*ck1+(Yistar(j,1)-yc1)*(sk1*co1+sp1*ck1*so1)+...
        (Zistar(j,1)-zc1)*(sk1*so1-sp1*ck1*co1);
    Vci1(j,1)=(Xistar(j,1)-xc1)*-cp1*sk1+(Yistar(j,1)-yc1)*(ck1*co1-sp1*sk1*so1)+...
        (Zistar(j,1)-zc1)*(ck1*so1+sp1*sk1*co1);
    Wci1(j,1)=(Xistar(j,1)-xc1)*sp1+(Yistar(j,1)-yc1)*-cp1*so1+(Zistar(j,1)-zc1)*cp1*co1;
end


for j=1:length
    uci1(j,1)=uc-f*(Uci1(j,1)/Wci1(j,1));
    vci1(j,1)=vc-f*(Vci1(j,1)/Wci1(j,1));
end


%Define postion and attitude of Camera 2
xc2=14; yc2=20; zc2=-40; phic2=0; kappac2=0; omegac2=45;
phic2=phic2*(pi/180); kappac2=kappac2*(pi/180);
omegac2=omegac2*(pi/180); cp2=cos(phic2); sp2=sin(phic2);
ck2=cos(kappac2); sk2=sin(kappac2); co2=cos(omegac2);
so2=sin(omegac2);

%Find target coords in camera frame
for j=1:length
    Uci2(j,1)=(Xistar(j,1)-xc2)*cp2*ck2+(Yistar(j,1)-yc2)*(sk2*co2+sp2*ck2*so2)+...
        (Zistar(j,1)-zc2)*(sk2*so2-sp2*ck2*co2);
    Vci2(j,1)=(Xistar(j,1)-xc2)*-cp2*sk2+(Yistar(j,1)-yc2)*(ck2*co2-sp2*sk2*so2)+...
        (Zistar(j,1)-zc2)*(ck2*so2+sp2*sk2*co2);
    Wci2(j,1)=(Xistar(j,1)-xc2)*sp2+(Yistar(j,1)-yc2)*-cp2*so2+(Zistar(j,1)-zc2)*cp2*co2;
end


for j=1:length
    uci2(j,1)=uc-f*(Uci2(j,1)/Wci2(j,1));
    vci2(j,1)=vc-f*(Vci2(j,1)/Wci2(j,1));
end


%Define postion and attitude of Camera 3
xc3=14; yc3=20; zc3=-20; phic3=0; kappac3=0; omegac3=90;
phic3=phic3*(pi/180); kappac3=kappac3*(pi/180);
omegac3=omegac3*(pi/180); cp3=cos(phic3); sp3=sin(phic3);
ck3=cos(kappac3); sk3=sin(kappac3); co3=cos(omegac3);
```

```
so3=sin(omegac3);

%Find target coords in camera frame
for j=1:length
    Uci3(j,1)=(Xistar(j,1)-xc3)*cp3*ck3+(Yistar(j,1)-yc3)*(sk3*co3+sp3*ck3*so3)+...
        (Zistar(j,1)-zc3)*(sk3*so3-sp3*ck3*co3);
    Vci3(j,1)=(Xistar(j,1)-xc3)*-cp3*sk3+(Yistar(j,1)-yc3)*(ck3*co3-sp3*sk3*so3)+...
        (Zistar(j,1)-zc3)*(ck3*so3+sp3*sk3*co3);
    Wci3(j,1)=(Xistar(j,1)-xc3)*sp3+(Yistar(j,1)-yc3)*-cp3*so3+(Zistar(j,1)-zc3)*cp3*co3;
end


for j=1:length
    uci3(j,1)=uc-f*(Uci3(j,1)/Wci3(j,1));
    vci3(j,1)=vc-f*(Vci3(j,1)/Wci3(j,1));
end


%Define postion and attitude of Camera 4
xc4=14; yc4=20; zc4=0; phic4=0; kappac4=0; omegac4=135;
phic4=phic4*(pi/180); kappac4=kappac4*(pi/180);
omegac4=omegac4*(pi/180); cp4=cos(phic4); sp4=sin(phic4);
ck4=cos(kappac4); sk4=sin(kappac4); co4=cos(omegac4);
so4=sin(omegac4);

%Find target coords in camera frame
for j=1:length
    Uci4(j,1)=(Xistar(j,1)-xc4)*cp4*ck4+(Yistar(j,1)-yc4)*(sk4*co4+sp4*ck4*so4)+...
        (Zistar(j,1)-zc4)*(sk4*so4-sp4*ck4*co4);
    Vci4(j,1)=(Xistar(j,1)-xc4)*-cp4*sk4+(Yistar(j,1)-yc4)*(ck4*co4-sp4*sk4*so4)+...
        (Zistar(j,1)-zc4)*(ck4*so4+sp4*sk4*co4);
    Wci4(j,1)=(Xistar(j,1)-xc4)*sp4+(Yistar(j,1)-yc4)*-cp4*so4+(Zistar(j,1)-zc4)*cp4*co4;
end


for j=1:length
    uci4(j,1)=uc-f*(Uci4(j,1)/Wci4(j,1));
    vci4(j,1)=vc-f*(Vci4(j,1)/Wci4(j,1));
end


%Define postion and attitude of Camera 5
xc5=14; yc5=0; zc5=0; phic5=0; kappac5=0; omegac5=180;
phic5=phic5*(pi/180); kappac5=kappac5*(pi/180);
omegac5=omegac5*(pi/180); cp5=cos(phic5); sp5=sin(phic5);
ck5=cos(kappac5); sk5=sin(kappac5); co5=cos(omegac5);
so5=sin(omegac5);
```

```
%Find target coords in camera frame
for j=1:length
   Uci5(j,1)=(Xistar(j,1)-xc5)*cp5*ck5+(Yistar(j,1)-yc5)*(sk5*co5+sp5*ck5*so5)+...
      (Zistar(j,1)-zc5)*(sk5*so5-sp5*ck5*co5);
   Vci5(j,1)=(Xistar(j,1)-xc5)*-cp5*sk5+(Yistar(j,1)-yc5)*(ck5*co5-sp5*sk5*so5)+...
      (Zistar(j,1)-zc5)*(ck5*so5+sp5*sk5*co5);
   Wci5(j,1)=(Xistar(j,1)-xc5)*sp5+(Yistar(j,1)-yc5)*-cp5*so5+(Zistar(j,1)-zc5)*cp5*co5;
end


for j=1:length
   uci5(j,1)=uc-f*(Uci5(j,1)/Wci5(j,1));
   vci5(j,1)=vc-f*(Vci5(j,1)/Wci5(j,1));
end


%Define postion and attitude of Camera 6
xc6=14; yc6=-20; zc6=0; phic6=0; kappac6=0; omegac6=225;
phic6=phic6*(pi/180); kappac6=kappac6*(pi/180);
omegac6=omegac6*(pi/180); cp6=cos(phic6); sp6=sin(phic6);
ck6=cos(kappac6); sk6=sin(kappac6); co6=cos(omegac6);
so6=sin(omegac6);


%Find target coords in camera frame
for j=1:length
   Uci6(j,1)=(Xistar(j,1)-xc6)*cp6*ck6+(Yistar(j,1)-yc6)*(sk6*co6+sp6*ck6*so6)+...
      (Zistar(j,1)-zc6)*(sk6*so6-sp6*ck6*co6);
   Vci6(j,1)=(Xistar(j,1)-xc6)*-cp6*sk6+(Yistar(j,1)-yc6)*(ck6*co6-sp6*sk6*so6)+...
      (Zistar(j,1)-zc6)*(ck6*so6+sp6*sk6*co6);
   Wci6(j,1)=(Xistar(j,1)-xc6)*sp6+(Yistar(j,1)-yc6)*-cp6*so6+(Zistar(j,1)-zc6)*cp6*co6;
end


for j=1:length
   uci6(j,1)=uc-f*(Uci6(j,1)/Wci6(j,1));
   vci6(j,1)=vc-f*(Vci6(j,1)/Wci6(j,1));
end


%Define postion and attitude of Camera 7
xc7=14; yc7=-20; zc7=-20; phic7=0; kappac7=0; omegac7=270;
phic7=phic7*(pi/180); kappac7=kappac7*(pi/180);
omegac7=omegac7*(pi/180); cp7=cos(phic7); sp7=sin(phic7);
ck7=cos(kappac7); sk7=sin(kappac7); co7=cos(omegac7);
so7=sin(omegac7);
```

```matlab
%Find target coords in camera frame
for j=1:length
    Uci7(j,1)=(Xistar(j,1)-xc7)*cp7*ck7+(Yistar(j,1)-yc7)*(sk7*co7+sp7*ck7*so7)+...
        (Zistar(j,1)-zc7)*(sk7*so7-sp7*ck7*co7);
    Vci7(j,1)=(Xistar(j,1)-xc7)*-cp7*sk7+(Yistar(j,1)-yc7)*(ck7*co7-sp7*sk7*so7)+...
        (Zistar(j,1)-zc7)*(ck7*so7+sp7*sk7*co7);
    Wci7(j,1)=(Xistar(j,1)-xc7)*sp7+(Yistar(j,1)-yc7)*-cp7*so7+(Zistar(j,1)-zc7)*cp7*co7;
end


for j=1:length
    uci7(j,1)=uc-f*(Uci7(j,1)/Wci7(j,1));
    vci7(j,1)=vc-f*(Vci7(j,1)/Wci7(j,1));
end


%Define postion and attitude of Camera 8
xc8=14; yc8=-20; zc8=-80; phic8=0; kappac8=0; omegac8=315;
phic8=phic8*(pi/180); kappac8=kappac8*(pi/180);
omegac8=omegac8*(pi/180); cp8=cos(phic8); sp8=sin(phic8);
ck8=cos(kappac8); sk8=sin(kappac8); co8=cos(omegac8);
so8=sin(omegac8);


%Find target coords in camera frame
for j=1:length
    Uci8(j,1)=(Xistar(j,1)-xc8)*cp8*ck8+(Yistar(j,1)-yc8)*(sk8*co8+sp8*ck8*so8)+...
        (Zistar(j,1)-zc8)*(sk8*so8-sp8*ck8*co8);
    Vci8(j,1)=(Xistar(j,1)-xc8)*-cp8*sk8+(Yistar(j,1)-yc8)*(ck8*co8-sp8*sk8*so8)+...
        (Zistar(j,1)-zc8)*(ck8*so8+sp8*sk8*co8);
    Wci8(j,1)=(Xistar(j,1)-xc8)*sp8+(Yistar(j,1)-yc8)*-cp8*so8+(Zistar(j,1)-zc8)*cp8*co8;
end


for j=1:length
    uci8(j,1)=uc-f*(Uci8(j,1)/Wci8(j,1));
    vci8(j,1)=vc-f*(Vci8(j,1)/Wci8(j,1));
end


%Plot Camera 1-4 perspective
figure(3),clf subplot(2,2,1), plot(vci1,uci1,'*') grid on
title('Camera 1') subplot(2,2,2), plot(vci2,uci2,'*') grid on
title('Camera 2') subplot(2,2,3), plot(vci3,uci3,'*') grid on
title('Camera 3') subplot(2,2,4), plot(vci4,uci4,'*') grid on
title('Camera 4')


%Plot Camera 5-8 perspective
```

```
figure(4),clf subplot(2,2,1), plot(vci5,uci5,'*') grid on
title('Camera 5') subplot(2,2,2), plot(vci6,uci6,'*') grid on
title('Camera 6') subplot(2,2,3), plot(vci7,uci7,'*') grid on
title('Camera 7') subplot(2,2,4), plot(vci8,uci8,'*') grid on
title('Camera 8')
```

Appendix B. Fortran Code

```
      program fit
ccccccccccccccccccccccccccccccccccccccccccccccccccccccc
c c              ***** COPYRIGHT NOTICE ***** c c
```

Subroutines in this file are based, in part, on the following c subroutines from Numerical Recipes in Fortran, Second Edition, c Cambridge University Press: c c   - CHOLDC: Cholesky decomposition of pos. def. sym. matrix c   - CHOLSL: Solution of associated linear system c   - MRQMIN: Levenberg-Marquardt nonlinear parameter optimization c   - MRQCOF: Calculate matrices and chi-square for MRQMIN c   - MRQSRT: Rearrangement of covariance matrix for MRQCOF c   - GASDEV: Randum number generator for Gaussian noise c   - RAN1:   Randum number generator for uniform noise c c   The following licence information and warranty disclaimer apply c   to the use of these routines: c

```
ccccccccccccccccccccccccccccccccccccccccccccccccccccccc
```

C C   Numerical Recipes Fortran Diskette Documentation v2.01 C C License Information and WARRANTY DISCLAIMER C C What does your license cover? C C   As the owner of this free Numerical Recipes diskette in IBM/PC C   format, you are licensed to install the programs on this diskette C   onto a single IBM/PC-compatible computer. You are not licensed C   to move the files to any other type of computer, nor to use them C   on more than a single IBM/PC-compatible computer for each diskette C purchased. By installing or using the programs, you acknowledge C acceptance of the following DISCLAIMER OF WARRANTY: C C DISCLAIMER OF WARRANTY C   THE PROGRAMS ACCESSED BY THIS ROUTINE (AND ON THE ORIGINAL C   DISKETTE) ARE PROVIDED   "AS IS"   WITHOUT WARRANTY OF ANY KIND. C   WE MAKE NO WARRANTIES, EXPRESS OR IMPLIED, THAT THEY ARE FREE OF C   ERROR,   OR ARE CONSISTENT WITH ANY PARTICULAR STANDARD OF C MERCHANTABILITY, OR THAT THEY WILL MEET YOUR REQUIREMENTS FOR ANY C   PARTICULAR APPLICATION. THEY SHOULD NOT BE RELIED ON FOR SOLVING C   A PROBLEM WHOSE INCORRECT SOLUTION   COULD   RESULT IN INJURY TO A C   PERSON OR LOSS OF PROPERTY. IF YOU DO USE THEM IN SUCH A MANNER, C   IT IS AT YOUR OWN RISK. THE AUTHORS AND PUBLISHER DISCLAIM ALL C   LIABILITY   FOR DIRECT,   INDIRECT, OR CONSEQUENTIAL DAMAGES C   RESULTING FROM YOUR USE OF THE PROGRAMS. C C   Can you redistribute Numerical Recipes in your programs? C C   If you want to include Numerical Recipes routines in programs that C   are further distributed (either commercially or non-commercially) C you can obtain permission to do so from Numerical Recipes Software. C If the routines are bound into your program executable and are not C separately visible to or useable by your users, there is generally C no charge, provided that (i) advance permission is obtained, and C (ii) a copyright notice like that on this diskette is embedded in C your program executable. Contact Numerical Recipes Software at C P.O. Box 243, Cambridge, MA 02238 (USA) [fax 617-863-1739] for C details. In distributing a program containing Numerical Recipes C routines, you acknowledge acceptance of the above DISCLAIMER OF C WARRANTY, and of the fact that no business relationship is created C between your program's users and Numerical Recipes Software, the C authors of the Numerical Recipes books, or Cambridge University C Press. C C If you want to distribute software that has Numerical Recipes in C the form of source code or individually callable object modules, C then you must contact Numerical Recipes Software for further C information. A fee (per Recipe) is charged, and we normally limit C the total number of Recipes distributed to 20. C C Licenses for other types of computers C C License information for other types of computers (including UNIX C workstations and servers, and multiple-user mainframes) is C available from Numerical Recipes Software (press F9 for address). C C For educational and noncommercial users, we offer two C ``streamlined'' procedures: C C Educational License for Single-Screen Workstation C C If you are affiliated with an educational or not-for-profit C research institution that is connected to the Internet, you may C license the programs for use on a single workstation (one C screen) as follows: Mail your name, address, and email address; C your workstation's hostname, internet address, brand and model C number; and a $50 one-time license fee (must accompany order) C to Numerical Recipes Software, at the address below (press F9). C Be sure to specify the language you want (FORTRAN or C). You will C receive, by return mail or email, instructions for downloading the C programs electronically. Upon payment of the fee you may also, if C you desire, upload the contents of this diskette (after unpacking C the files with the NRCOPY program) to your workstation. C C Right-to-Copy License for Courses C C Instructors at accredited educational institutions who have C adopted Numerical Recipes for a course, and who already own a C diskette, may license the programs for use in that course as C follows: Mail your name, title, and address; the course name, C number, dates, and

estimated enrollment; and advance payment of C $5 per
(estimated) student to Numerical Recipes Software, at the C
address below (F9). You will receive by return mail a license C
authorizing you to make copies of your diskette for use by your C
students, and/or to transfer the programs to a machine C
accessible to your students (but only for the duration of the C
course). C C   How to contact Numerical Recipes Software
C C   Our address is: Numerical Recipes Software C
P.O. Box 243 C   Cambridge, MA 02238 (USA) C C
Our fax number is: 617-863-1739. C C   Sorry, we do not take
telephone calls other than fax. C
ccccccccccccccccccccccccccccccccccccccccccccccccccccccc

```
      ! Variables associated with target points (corners of cube):
!     parameter (nmax=8)
      real x(5000),y(5000),z(5000)      ! Model coordinates
      real xU(5000),yU(5000),zU(5000)   ! Unbent Model coordinates
      real xt(5000),yt(5000),zt(5000)   ! Tunnel coordinates
      real u(5000),v(5000)              ! Image coordinates
      real u2(5000),v2(5000)            ! Image coordinates
      real u3(5000),v3(5000)            ! Image coordinates
      real u4(5000),v4(5000)            ! Image coordinates
   real Xmax(5000)                      ! Distance from midline to leading edge


   ! Wing frame displacement from model frame
   real DDX,DDY


   ! Chord length of wing
   real Ymax,xmid,div,TA,w,tip,xf,yf,xtip,ytip


      ! Variables associated with camera (star superscript not shown):
      real phic,phic2,kappac,kappac2,omegac,omegac2,bc,tc,
     *     phic3,kappac3,omegac3,phic4,kappac4,omegac4
   integer nmax
   common /camera/ uc,vc,fc,xc,yc,zc,xc2,yc2,zc2,xc3,yc3,zc3,
     *   xc4,yc4,zc4,uxc,uyc,uzc,vxc,vyc,vzc,wxc,wyc,wzc,
     *   uxc2,uyc2,uzc2,vxc2,vyc2,vzc2,wxc2,wyc2,wzc2,
     *   uxc3,uyc3,uzc3,vxc3,vyc3,vzc3,wxc3,wyc3,wzc3,
     *   uxc4,uyc4,uzc4,vxc4,vyc4,vzc4,wxc4,wyc4,wzc4


   ! Variables associated with position and attitude:
   parameter (npar=8)
   real posatt(npar),fitrms(npar)
```

```fortran
c.... Degrees/radians conversion:
      raddeg = atan(1.)/45.

c.... Assume target points on corners of cube: !      data x
    /12.,12.,0.,0.,12.,12.,0.,0./ !     data y
    /0.,12.,12.,0.,0.,12.,12.,0./ !     data z
    /0.,0.,0.,0.,12.,12.,12.,12./

 100  FORMAT(I5)
 200  FORMAT(3(F16.12))
 300  FORMAT(F16.12,3X,F16.12,3X,F16.12)
 400  FORMAT(F5.5)
      open(2,FILE='data.in',STATUS='OLD')
      read(2,100) nmax
      read(2,400) bc
      read(2,400) tc
      read(2,400) DDX
      read(2,400) DDY
      read(2,400) Ymax
        DO I=1,nmax
          read(2,200) x(I),y(I),z(I)
        ENDDO
        DO I=1,nmax
          read(2,200) xU(I),yU(I),zU(I)
        ENDDO

        write(3,100) nmax
      write(3,*) bc
      write(3,*) tc
      write(3,*) DDX
      write(3,*) DDY
      write(3,*) Ymax
        DO I=1,nmax
          write(3,300) x(I),y(I),z(I)
      enddo
        DO I=1,nmax
          write(3,300) xU(I),yU(I),zU(I)
      enddo

c.... Calculate angle of twist axis, given undeformed coords
      ! This assumes that the origin of the wing frame is centered
      ! at the point of attachment of the fuselage
      xmid = 0.
```

```
          div = 0.
          do i=1,nmax
              w = yU(i)-DDY
              tip = yU(nmax)-DDY
              if (w.EQ.tip) then
                  xmid = xmid + xU(i)-DDX
                  div = div + 1
              endif
          enddo
          xmid = xmid/div
          TA = atan(xmid/Ymax)

c.... Input coords of leading edge endpoints, in wing frame
          xf=4.925
          yf=0.
          xtip=-1.177
          ytip=6.78

c.... Calculate Xmax for each Y along the wing
          do i=1,nmax
              Xmax(i)=((xtip-xf)/(ytip-yf))*(yU(i)-DDY)+xf
          enddo
          do i=1,nmax
              Xmax(i)=Xmax(i)*cos(TA)-(yU(i)-DDY)*sin(TA)
          enddo

c.... Specify the camera parameters:
          uc = 512.   ! pixels
          vc = 512.   ! pixels
          fc = 1000.  ! pixels
          xc = 14.
          yc = 0.
          zc = -40.
          phic = 0.     ! degrees
          kappac = 0.   ! degrees
          omegac = 0.   ! degrees

          xc2 = 14.
          yc2 = 20.
          zc2 = -40.
          phic2 = 0.     ! degrees
          kappac2 = 0.   ! degrees
          omegac2 = -45. ! degrees
```

```
      xc3 = 14.
       yc3 = 20.
       zc3 = -20.
       phic3 = 0.      ! degrees
       kappac3 = 0.    ! degrees
       omegac3 = -90.  ! degrees

      xc4 = 14.
       yc4 = 20.
       zc4 = 0.
       phic4 = 0.      ! degrees
       kappac4 = 0.    ! degrees
       omegac4 = -135. ! degrees

c.... Convert angles to radians:
       phic = phic*raddeg
       kappac = kappac*raddeg
       omegac = omegac*raddeg
       phic2 = phic2*raddeg
       kappac2 = kappac2*raddeg
       omegac2 = omegac2*raddeg
       phic3 = phic3*raddeg
       kappac3 = kappac3*raddeg
       omegac3 = omegac3*raddeg
       phic4 = phic4*raddeg
       kappac4 = kappac4*raddeg
       omegac4 = omegac4*raddeg

c.... Calculate the camera orientation matrices:
       call setmatrix (phic,kappac,omegac,
     *   uxc,uyc,uzc,vxc,vyc,vzc,wxc,wyc,wzc)
       call setmatrix (phic2,kappac2,omegac2,
     *   uxc2,uyc2,uzc2,vxc2,vyc2,vzc2,wxc2,wyc2,wzc2)
       call setmatrix (phic3,kappac3,omegac3,
     *   uxc3,uyc3,uzc3,vxc3,vyc3,vzc3,wxc3,wyc3,wzc3)
       call setmatrix (phic4,kappac4,omegac4,
     *   uxc4,uyc4,uzc4,vxc4,vyc4,vzc4,wxc4,wyc4,wzc4)

c.... Specify position and attitude of test article:
       dxk = 5
       dyk = 0
       dzk = -20
```

```
            alphak = 15.*raddeg
            betak  = 10.*raddeg
            phik   = 5.*raddeg

c.... Calculate tunnel coordinates of targets:
            call setmatrix (alphak,betak,phik,
     *         r11,r12,r13,r21,r22,r23,r31,r32,r33)
            do i = 1, nmax
                xt(i) = dxk + r11*x(i) + r12*y(i) + r13*z(i)
                yt(i) = dyk + r21*x(i) + r22*y(i) + r23*z(i)
                zt(i) = dzk + r31*x(i) + r32*y(i) + r33*z(i)
            enddo

c.... Specify noise level on image coordinates:
            spread = .00001 ! pixel
            idum = -911 ! initialie seed for random number generator

c.... Calculate corresponding image coordinates:
            open(1,FILE='fit.out',STATUS='UNKNOWN')
            write(1,*)
            write(1,*) '... Synthetic input data including noise:'
            write(1,*)
        write(1,*) 'Camera 1:'
        write(1,"(a)") '    i       u(i)      v(i)'
            do i = 1, nmax
                uki = uxc*(xt(i)-xc) + uyc*(yt(i)-yc) + uzc*(zt(i)-zc)
                vki = vxc*(xt(i)-xc) + vyc*(yt(i)-yc) + vzc*(zt(i)-zc)
                wki = wxc*(xt(i)-xc) + wyc*(yt(i)-yc) + wzc*(zt(i)-zc)
c               write(*,*) uki,vki,wki
                u(i) = uc - fc*uki/wki + spread*gasdev(idum)
                v(i) = vc - fc*vki/wki + spread*gasdev(idum)
                write(1,"(i4,2f9.3)") i, u(i), v(i)
            enddo
        write(1,*)
        write(1,*) 'Camera 2:'
          write(1,"(a)") '    i       u(i)      v(i)'
            do i = 1, nmax
                uki2 = uxc2*(xt(i)-xc2) + uyc2*(yt(i)-yc2) + uzc2*(zt(i)-zc2)
                vki2 = vxc2*(xt(i)-xc2) + vyc2*(yt(i)-yc2) + vzc2*(zt(i)-zc2)
                wki2 = wxc2*(xt(i)-xc2) + wyc2*(yt(i)-yc2) + wzc2*(zt(i)-zc2)
                u2(i) = uc - fc*uki2/wki2 + spread*gasdev(idum)
                v2(i) = vc - fc*vki2/wki2 + spread*gasdev(idum)
                write(1,"(i4,2f9.3)") i, u2(i), v2(i)
```

```
          enddo
      write(1,*)
      write(1,*) 'Camera 3:'
         write(1,"(a)") '   i     u(i)     v(i)'
         do i = 1, nmax
            uki3 = uxc3*(xt(i)-xc3) + uyc3*(yt(i)-yc3) + uzc3*(zt(i)-zc3)
            vki3 = vxc3*(xt(i)-xc3) + vyc3*(yt(i)-yc3) + vzc3*(zt(i)-zc3)
            wki3 = wxc3*(xt(i)-xc3) + wyc3*(yt(i)-yc3) + wzc3*(zt(i)-zc3)
            u3(i) = uc - fc*uki3/wki3 + spread*gasdev(idum)
            v3(i) = vc - fc*vki3/wki3 + spread*gasdev(idum)
            write(1,"(i4,2f9.3)") i, u3(i), v3(i)
         enddo
      write(1,*)
      write(1,*) 'Camera 4:'
         write(1,"(a)") '   i     u(i)     v(i)'
         do i = 1, nmax
            uki4 = uxc4*(xt(i)-xc4) + uyc4*(yt(i)-yc4) + uzc4*(zt(i)-zc4)
            vki4 = vxc4*(xt(i)-xc4) + vyc4*(yt(i)-yc4) + vzc4*(zt(i)-zc4)
            wki4 = wxc4*(xt(i)-xc4) + wyc4*(yt(i)-yc4) + wzc4*(zt(i)-zc4)
            u4(i) = uc - fc*uki4/wki4 + spread*gasdev(idum)
            v4(i) = vc - fc*vki4/wki4 + spread*gasdev(idum)
            write(1,"(i4,2f9.3)") i, u4(i), v4(i)
         enddo

c.... Initialize the least-squares fit:
      do ipar = 1, npar
         posatt(ipar) = 0. ! initial guess for pos&att values
      enddo

c.... Estimate the noise level (in this case known exactly):
      sigma = spread

c.... Perform the fit:
      call pafit (nmax,x,y,z,xU,yU,zU,u,v,u2,v2,u3,v3,u4,v4,
     *sigma,posatt,fitrms,rmspix,TA,Xmax,Ymax,DDX,DDY)

c.... Report results:
      write(1,*)
      write(1,*) '... Final results of LM fit: '
      write(1,"(1x,a)")
     *  '                 FIT     EXACT     ERROR    PRECISION'
      write(1,"(1x,a,4f10.5)") 'DeltaX_k:',
     *  posatt(1), dxk, posatt(1)-dxk, fitrms(1)
```

```fortran
      write(1,"(1x,a,4f10.5)") 'DeltaY_k:',
     *  posatt(2), dyk, posatt(2)-dyk, fitrms(2)
      write(1,"(1x,a,4f10.5)") 'DeltaZ_k:',
     *  posatt(3), dzk, posatt(3)-dzk, fitrms(3)
      write(1,"(1x,a,4f10.5)") ' Alpha_k:',
     *  posatt(4)/raddeg, alphak/raddeg, (posatt(4)-alphak)/raddeg,
     *  fitrms(4)/raddeg
      write(1,"(1x,a,4f10.5)") '  Beta_k:',
     *  posatt(5)/raddeg, betak/raddeg, (posatt(5)-betak)/raddeg,
     *  fitrms(5)/raddeg
      write(1,"(1x,a,4f10.5)") '   Phi_k:',
     *  posatt(6)/raddeg, phik/raddeg, (posatt(6)-phik)/raddeg,
     *  fitrms(6)/raddeg
      write(1,"(1x,a,4f10.5)") '      BC:',
     *  posatt(7), bc, posatt(7)-bc, fitrms(7)
      write(1,"(1x,a,4f10.5)") '      TC:',
     *  posatt(8), tc, posatt(8)-tc, fitrms(8)

c.... Compare calculated and actual noise:
      write(1,*)
      write(1,*) '... Compare calculated and actual noise amplitude: '
      write(1,"(1x,a)") 'CALCULATED    ACTUAL'
      write(1,"(1x,2f10.5)") rmspix, spread

      open(7,FILE='ERROR.out',STATUS='UNKNOWN')
      write(7,*) posatt(1)-dxk
      write(7,*) posatt(2)-dyk
      write(7,*) posatt(3)-dzk
      write(7,*) (posatt(4)-alphak)/raddeg
      write(7,*) (posatt(5)-betak)/raddeg
      write(7,*) (posatt(6)-phik)/raddeg
      write(7,*) posatt(7)-bc
      write(7,*) posatt(8)-tc
      end

ccccccccccccccccccccccccccccccccccccccccccccccccccccccccccccc

      ! From Ruyten, Appendix B, Eq.(B-1)

      subroutine setmatrix (alpha,beta,phi,
     *  r11,r12,r13,r21,r22,r23,r31,r32,r33)

      ca = cos(alpha)
```

```fortran
      sa = sin(alpha)
      cb = cos(beta)
      sb = sin(beta)
      cp = cos(phi)
      sp = sin(phi)

      sasp = sa*sp
      sacp = sa*cp

      r11 = ca*cb
      r12 = sb*cp + sasp*cb
      r13 = -sb*sp + sacp*cb
      r21 = -ca*sb
      r22 = cb*cp - sasp*sb
      r23 = -cb*sp - sacp*sb
      r31 = -sa
      r32 = ca*sp
      r33 = ca*cp

      end
```

```
cccccccccccccccccccccccccccccccccccccccccccccccccccccccccccccccc

      subroutine pafit (nmax,x,y,z,xU,yU,zU,u,v,u2,v2,u3,v3,u4,v4,
     *sigma,posatt,fitrms,rmspix,TA,Xmax,Ymax,DDX,DDY)

      real x(*),y(*),z(*),u(*),v(*),u2(*),v2(*),posatt(*),fitrms(*),
     *xU(*),yU(*),zU(*),u3(*),v3(*),u4(*),v4(*),Xmax(*)

      parameter (npar=8)
      real coef(npar),covar(npar,npar),alfa(npar,npar)
      integer ifit(npar)

c.... Convergence criteria for LM optimization:
      dcmin = 0.01
      nconv = 4

c.... Initialize parameters:
      do ipar = 1, npar
         coef(ipar) = posatt(ipar)
         ifit(ipar) = 0
      enddo
```

```
c.... Initialize Levenberg-Marquardt:
      alambda = -1.
      call mrqmin1 (nmax,x,y,z,xU,yU,zU,u,v,u2,v2,u3,v3,u4,v4,
     *sigma,coef,ifit,covar,alfa,npar,chisq,alambda,nfree,TA,Xmax,
     *Ymax,DDX,DDY)

c.... Iterate Levenberg-Marquardt to convergence:
      ktot = 1
      knew = 0
      write(1,*)
      write(1,*) '... Progress of LM fit:'
      write(1,*) 'ITER        CHISQ        RMSPIX       LAMBDA'
      do while (knew.lt.nconv)
         rmspix = sigma * sqrt(chisq/float(nmax))
         write(1,"(i5,1p,9e12.3)") ktot, chisq, rmspix, alambda
         ktot = ktot + 1
         ochisq = chisq
         call mrqmin1 (nmax,x,y,z,xU,yU,zU,u,v,u2,v2,u3,v3,u4,v4,
     *   sigma,coef,ifit,covar,alfa,npar,chisq,alambda,nfree,TA,Xmax,
     *   Ymax,DDX,DDY)
         if (chisq.gt.ochisq) then
            knew = 0
         elseif (abs(ochisq-chisq).lt.dcmin) then
            knew = knew + 1
         endif
      enddo

c.... Transfer parameters back to posatt:
      do ipar = 1, npar
         posatt(ipar) = coef(ipar)
      enddo

c.... Calculate precision:
      alambda = 0.
      call mrqmin1 (nmax,x,y,z,xU,yU,zU,u,v,u2,v2,u3,v3,u4,v4,
     *   sigma,coef,ifit,covar,alfa,npar,chisq,alambda,nfree,TA,Xmax,
     *   Ymax,DDX,DDY)
      sigsca = sqrt(chisq/float(nfree))
      do ipar = 1, npar
         fitrms(ipar) = sigsca*sqrt(covar(ipar,ipar))
      enddo

      end
```

```fortran
ccccccccccccccccccccccccccccccccccccccccccccccccccccc
c c     Substantial modifications have been made to the routines c
MRQMIN, MRQCOF, and MRQSRT: c c     1. Replaced
x(*),y(*),sig(*),ndata in calling sequence c       with alternate
pass-through argument lists c    2. Using scalar sigma instead of
vector. c    3. Replaced ma and nca in argument lists with npar.
c    4. Returning number of degrees of freedom: nfree. c    5.
Removed external reference to funcs. c    6. Replaced gaussj with
choldc, cholsl. c    7. Replaced covsrt with makecovar: See
makecovar. c    8. Changed from y=y(xi,a) to u=u(i,a) + v=v(i,a).
c    9. Calling functions mrqfun: initial call to set parameters.
c    10. Changed ia=0 to signify fitting parameter. c
ccccccccccccccccccccccccccccccccccccccccccccccccccccc
c c     Adaptation of Numerical Recipes "covsrt". Based on
Cholesky c    decomposition of covar: adapted calculation of L^-1
from c    Num. Rec. p91. Results checked against gaussj --> OK. c
      subroutine makecovar (covar,alpha,pivot,ifix,maxpar,npar,mfit)

      real covar(maxpar,maxpar),alpha(maxpar,maxpar),pivot(*)
      integer ifix(*)

      ! Determine L^-1 according to Num. Rec. p91:
      do i = 1, mfit
         covar(i,i) = 1./pivot(i)
         do j = i+1, mfit
            sum = 0.
            do k = i, j-1
               sum = sum - covar(j,k)*covar(k,i)
            enddo
            covar(j,i) = sum/pivot(j)
         enddo
      enddo

      ! Form covar = (L^-1)^T (L^-1)'
      do i = 1, mfit
         do j = i, mfit
            sum = 0.
            do k = max(i,j), mfit
               sum = sum + covar(k,i)*covar(k,j)
            enddo
            alpha(i,j) = sum
            alpha(j,i) = sum
```

```
            enddo
        enddo

        ! Set remainder of matrix to zero:
        do i = mfit+1, npar
            do j = 1, i
                alpha(i,j) = 0.
                alpha(j,i) = 0.
            enddo
        enddo

        ! Copy from alpha to covar:
        do i = 1, npar
            do j = 1, npar
                covar(i,j) = alpha(i,j)
            enddo
        enddo

        ! Redistribute:
        k = mfit
        do j = npar, 1, -1
            if (ifix(j).eq.0) then
                do i = 1, npar
                    swap = covar(i,k)
                    covar(i,k) = covar(i,j)
                    covar(i,j) = swap
                enddo
                do i = 1, npar
                    swap = covar(k,i)
                    covar(k,i) = covar(j,i)
                    covar(j,i) = swap
                enddo
                k = k - 1
            endif
        enddo

        end
ccccccccccccccccccccccccccccccccccccccccccccccccccccccc

        SUBROUTINE mrqmin1 (nmax,x,y,z,xU,yU,zU,u,v,u2,v2,u3,v3,u4,v4,
     *  sigma,a,ifix,covar,alpha,npar,chisq,alambda,nfree,TA,Xmax,
     *  Ymax,DDX,DDY)
```

B-13

```fortran
      real x(*),y(*),z(*),xU(*),yU(*),zU(*),u(*),v(*),u2(*),v2(*),
     *   u3(*),v3(*),u4(*),v4(*),Xmax(*)

      INTEGER ifix(npar)
      REAL a(npar),alpha(npar,npar),covar(npar,npar)

      PARAMETER (MMAX=8)
      REAL atry(MMAX),beta(MMAX),da(MMAX), pivot(MMAX)

      SAVE ochisq,atry,beta,da,mfit

      if (npar.gt.MMAX) stop '*** mrqmin1: npar.gt.MMAX ***'

      if (alambda.lt.0.) then
         mfit = 0
         do j = 1, npar
            if (ifix(j).eq.0) mfit = mfit + 1
         enddo
         alambda = 0.001

         call mrqcof1 (nmax,x,y,z,xU,yU,zU,u,v,u2,v2,u3,v3,u4,v4,
     *   sigma,a,ifix,alpha,beta,npar,chisq,nfree,TA,Xmax,Ymax,DDX,DDY)
         ochisq = chisq
         do j = 1, npar
            atry(j) = a(j)
         enddo
      endif

      j = 0
      do l = 1, npar
         if (ifix(l).eq.0) then
            j = j + 1
            k = 0
            do m = 1, npar
               if (ifix(m).eq.0) then
                  k = k + 1
                  covar(j,k) = alpha(j,k)
               endif
            enddo
            covar(j,j) = alpha(j,j)*(1.+alambda)
            da(j) = beta(j)
         endif
```

```fortran
        enddo

        ! Prepare for linear system solution or matrix inverse:
        open(4,FILE='Amatrix.out',STATUS='UNKNOWN')
        write(4,*) covar
write(4,*)
        call choldc (covar,mfit,npar,pivot,ierr)

        ! Compute covariance matrix (was: "covsrt"):
        if (alambda.eq.0.) then
           call makecovar (covar,alpha,pivot,ifix,npar,npar,mfit)
           return
        endif

        ! Proceed with solution of linear system:
        call cholsl (covar,mfit,npar,pivot,da,da)
        j = 0
        do l = 1, npar
           if (ifix(l).eq.0) then
              j = j + 1
              atry(l) = a(l) + da(j)
           endif
        enddo

        call mrqcof1 (nmax,x,y,z,xU,yU,zU,u,v,u2,v2,u3,v3,u4,v4,
     *    sigma,atry,ifix,covar,da,npar,chisq,nfree,TA,Xmax,Ymax,DDX,DDY)

        if (chisq.lt.ochisq) then
           alambda = 0.1*alambda
           ochisq = chisq
           j = 0
           do l = 1, npar
              if (ifix(l).eq.0) then
                 j = j + 1
                 k = 0
                 do m = 1, npar
                    if (ifix(m).eq.0) then
                       k = k + 1
                       alpha(j,k) = covar(j,k)
                    endif
                 enddo
                 beta(j) = da(j)
                 a(l) = atry(l)
```

```fortran
              endif
           enddo
        else
           alambda = 10.*alambda
           chisq = ochisq
        endif

        END

C  (C) Copr. 1986-92 Numerical Recipes Software ~-259u.. c
Modified by W. M. Ruyten

ccccccccccccccccccccccccccccccccccccccccccccccccccccccccc

        SUBROUTINE mrqcof1 (nmax,x,y,z,xU,yU,zU,u,v,u2,v2,u3,v3,u4,v4,
     *   sigma,a,ifix,alpha,beta,npar,chisq,nfree,TA,Xmax,Ymax,DDX,DDY)

        real x(*),y(*),z(*),xU(*),yU(*),zU(*),u(*),v(*),u2(*),v2(*),
     *u3(*),v3(*),u4(*),v4(*),Xmax(*)

        INTEGER ifix(npar)
        REAL a(npar),alpha(npar,npar),beta(npar)

        PARAMETER (MMAX=8)
        REAL duda(MMAX),dvda(MMAX),duda2(MMAX),dvda2(MMAX)
        REAL duda3(MMAX),dvda3(MMAX),duda4(MMAX),dvda4(MMAX)

        if (npar.gt.MMAX) stop '*** mrqcof1: npar.gt.MMAX ***'

c.... Initialize arrays:
        mfit = 0
        do j = 1, npar
           if (ifix(j).eq.0) mfit = mfit + 1
        enddo
        do j = 1, mfit
           do k = 1, j
              alpha(j,k) = 0.
           enddo
           beta(j) = 0.
        enddo

c.... Initialize rotation matrix and derivative:
        i = 0
```

```
          call mrqfun1 (i,x,y,z,xU,yU,zU,a,upred,upred2,vpred,vpred2,
         *upred3,upred4,vpred3,vpred4,duda,duda2,duda3,duda4,dvda,
         *dvda2,dvda3,dvda4,TA,Xmax,Ymax,DDX,DDY)

c.... Build alpha and beta by summing over all points:
          chisq = 0.
          do i = 1, nmax

          call mrqfun1 (i,x,y,z,xU,yU,zU,a,upred,upred2,vpred,vpred2,
         *upred3,upred4,vpred3,vpred4,duda,duda2,duda3,duda4,dvda,
         *dvda2,dvda3,dvda4,TA,Xmax,Ymax,DDX,DDY)

             du  = u(i)  - upred
             dv  = v(i)  - vpred
             du2 = u2(i) - upred2
             dv2 = v2(i) - vpred2
             du3 = u3(i) - upred3
             dv3 = v3(i) - vpred3
             du4 = u4(i) - upred4
             dv4 = v4(i) - vpred4

            j = 0
            do l = 1, npar
               if (ifix(l).eq.0) then
                  j = j + 1
                  wtu  = duda(l)
                  wtv  = dvda(l)
                  wtu2 = duda2(l)
                  wtv2 = dvda2(l)
                  wtu3 = duda3(l)
                  wtv3 = dvda3(l)
                  wtu4 = duda4(l)
                  wtv4 = dvda4(l)

                  k = 0
                  do m = 1, l
                     if (ifix(m).eq.0) then
                        k = k + 1
                        alpha(j,k) = alpha(j,k)
     *                     + wtu*duda(m)   + wtv*dvda(m)
     *                     + wtu2*duda2(m) + wtv2*dvda2(m)
     *                     + wtu3*duda3(m) + wtv3*dvda3(m)
     *                     + wtu4*duda4(m) + wtv4*dvda4(m)
```

```
                endif
             enddo
             beta(j) = beta(j) + du*wtu + dv*wtv
     *                       + du2*wtu2 + dv2*wtv2
     *                       + du3*wtu3 + dv3*wtv3
     *                       + du4*wtu4 + dv4*wtv4
          endif
       enddo
       chisq = chisq + du*du + dv*dv + du2*du2 + dv2*dv2
     *              + du3*du3 + dv3*dv3 + du4*du4 + dv4*dv4

    enddo
c.... Perform scaling by sigma:
    sig2i = 1./(sigma*sigma)
    do j = 1, mfit
       do k = 1, j
          alpha(j,k) = alpha(j,k)*sig2i
       enddo
       beta(j) = beta(j)*sig2i
    enddo
    chisq = chisq*sig2i

c.... Fill out matrix:
    do j = 2, mfit
       do k = 1, j-1
          alpha(k,j) = alpha(j,k)
       enddo
    enddo

c.... Determine number of degrees of freedom:
    nfree = 2*nmax - mfit

    END


C  (C) Copr. 1986-92 Numerical Recipes Software ~-259u.. c
Modified by W. M. Ruyten

ccccccccccccccccccccccccccccccccccccccccccccccccccccccc

    SUBROUTINE mrqfun1 (i,x,y,z,xU,yU,zU,coef,upred,upred2,vpred,
   *vpred2,upred3,upred4,vpred3,vpred4,duda,duda2,duda3,duda4,dvda,
   *dvda2,dvda3,dvda4,TA,Xmax,Ymax,DDX,DDY)
```

```fortran
      real x(*),y(*),z(*),xU(*),yU(*),zU(*),Xmax(*),maxX

      REAL coef(*), duda(*),dvda(*),duda2(*),dvda2(*)
      REAL duda3(*),dvda3(*),duda4(*),dvda4(*)

      save dx,dy,dz, r11,r12,r13,r21,r22,r23,r31,r32,r33, sb,cb

      ! Camera common block copied from top of program
      common /camera/ uc,vc,fc,xc,yc,zc,xc2,yc2,zc2,xc3,yc3,zc3,
     *    xc4,yc4,zc4,uxc,uyc,uzc,vxc,vyc,vzc,wxc,wyc,wzc,
     *    uxc2,uyc2,uzc2,vxc2,vyc2,vzc2,wxc2,wyc2,wzc2,
     *    uxc3,uyc3,uzc3,vxc3,vyc3,vzc3,wxc3,wyc3,wzc3,
     *    uxc4,uyc4,uzc4,vxc4,vyc4,vzc4,wxc4,wyc4,wzc4

c.... Calculate trig factors only on initial call:
      if (i.gt.0) goto 10

      dx = coef(1)
      dy = coef(2)
      dz = coef(3)

      alpha = coef(4)
      beta = coef(5)
      phi = coef(6)

    BC = coef(7)
    TC = coef(8)

      ca = cos(alpha)
      sa = sin(alpha)
      cb = cos(beta)
      sb = sin(beta)
      cp = cos(phi)
      sp = sin(phi)

      sasp = sa*sp
      sacp = sa*cp

      r11 = ca*cb
      r12 = sb*cp + sasp*cb
      r13 = -sb*sp + sacp*cb
      r21 = -ca*sb
      r22 = cb*cp - sasp*sb
```

```
      r23 = -cb*sp - sacp*sb
      r31 = -sa
      r32 = ca*sp
      r33 = ca*cp

      return

c.... Perform actual calculation: 10    xi = xU(i)
      yi = yU(i)
      zi = zU(i)

      xtw = (xU(i)-DDX)*cos(TA) - (yU(i)-DDY)*sin(TA)
      ytw = (xU(i)-DDX)*sin(TA) + (yU(i)-DDY)*cos(TA)
      maxX = Xmax(i)

        ! Tunnel coordinates of targets:
      xt = dx + r11*xi + r12*yi + r13*((-BC)*((yi-DDY)/Ymax)*
     *      ((yi-DDY)/Ymax)+TC*(ytw/Ymax)*(xtw/maxX))
      yt = dy + r21*xi + r22*yi + r23*((-BC)*((yi-DDY)/Ymax)*
     *      ((yi-DDY)/Ymax)+TC*(ytw/Ymax)*(xtw/maxX))
      zt = dz + r31*xi + r32*yi + r33*((-BC)*((yi-DDY)/Ymax)*
     *      ((yi-DDY)/Ymax)+TC*(ytw/Ymax)*(xtw/maxX))

        ! Implied image coordinates:
      uki = uxc*(xt-xc) + uyc*(yt-yc) + uzc*(zt-zc)
      open(5,FILE='duda.out',STATUS='UNKNOWN')
      write(5,*)i
      write(5,*)maxX
      vki = vxc*(xt-xc) + vyc*(yt-yc) + vzc*(zt-zc)
      wki = wxc*(xt-xc) + wyc*(yt-yc) + wzc*(zt-zc)
      upred = uc - fc*uki/wki
      vpred = vc - fc*vki/wki

      uki2 = uxc2*(xt-xc2) + uyc2*(yt-yc2) + uzc2*(zt-zc2)
      vki2 = vxc2*(xt-xc2) + vyc2*(yt-yc2) + vzc2*(zt-zc2)
      wki2 = wxc2*(xt-xc2) + wyc2*(yt-yc2) + wzc2*(zt-zc2)
      upred2 = uc - fc*uki2/wki2
      vpred2 = vc - fc*vki2/wki2

      uki3 = uxc3*(xt-xc3) + uyc3*(yt-yc3) + uzc3*(zt-zc3)
      vki3 = vxc3*(xt-xc3) + vyc3*(yt-yc3) + vzc3*(zt-zc3)
      wki3 = wxc3*(xt-xc3) + wyc3*(yt-yc3) + wzc3*(zt-zc3)
      upred3 = uc - fc*uki3/wki3
```

```
          vpred3 = vc - fc*vki3/wki3

          uki4 = uxc4*(xt-xc4) + uyc4*(yt-yc4) + uzc4*(zt-zc4)
          vki4 = vxc4*(xt-xc4) + vyc4*(yt-yc4) + vzc4*(zt-zc4)
          wki4 = wxc4*(xt-xc4) + wyc4*(yt-yc4) + wzc4*(zt-zc4)
          upred4 = uc - fc*uki4/wki4
          vpred4 = vc - fc*vki4/wki4

c.... Calculate partial derivatives w.r.t. fit parameters:

          ! Use trick for derivatives w.r.t. alpha_k:
          ! (dR/dalpha_k)*(R^T) = (0,0,cb, 0,0,-sb, -cb,sb,0)

          ! Start with tunnel coordinates:
          dxt1 = 1.
          dxt2 = 0.
          dxt3 = 0.
          dxt4 = cb*(zt-dz)
          dxt5 = (yt-dy)
          dxt6 = r13*yi - r12*((-BC)*((yi-DDY)/Ymax)*((yi-DDY)/Ymax)+
     *           TC*(ytw/Ymax)*(xtw/maxX))
          dxt7 = -r13*((yi-DDY)/Ymax)*((yi-DDY)/Ymax)
          dxt8 = r13*(ytw/Ymax)*(xtw/maxX)

          dyt1 = 0.
          dyt2 = 1.
          dyt3 = 0.
          dyt4 = -sb*(zt-dz)
          dyt5 = -(xt-dx)
          dyt6 = r23*yi - r22*((-BC)*((yi-DDY)/Ymax)*((yi-DDY)/Ymax)+
     *           TC*(ytw/Ymax)*(xtw/maxX))
          dyt7 = -r23*((yi-DDY)/Ymax)*((yi-DDY)/Ymax)
          dyt8 = r23*(ytw/Ymax)*(xtw/maxX)

          dzt1 = 0.
          dzt2 = 0.
          dzt3 = 1.
          dzt4 = -cb*(xt-dx) + sb*(yt-dy)
          dzt5 = 0.
          dzt6 = r33*yi - r32*((-BC)*((yi-DDY)/Ymax)*((yi-DDY)/Ymax)+
     *           TC*(ytw/Ymax)*(xtw/maxX))
          dzt7 = -r33*((yi-DDY)/Ymax)*((yi-DDY)/Ymax)
          dzt8 = r33*(ytw/Ymax)*(xtw/maxX)
```

```
! Continue by chain rule with U,V,W product terms:
duki1a = uxc*dxt1 + uyc*dyt1 + uzc*dzt1
duki2a = uxc*dxt2 + uyc*dyt2 + uzc*dzt2
duki3a = uxc*dxt3 + uyc*dyt3 + uzc*dzt3
duki4a = uxc*dxt4 + uyc*dyt4 + uzc*dzt4
duki5a = uxc*dxt5 + uyc*dyt5 + uzc*dzt5
duki6a = uxc*dxt6 + uyc*dyt6 + uzc*dzt6
duki7a = uxc*dxt7 + uyc*dyt7 + uzc*dzt7
duki8a = uxc*dxt8 + uyc*dyt8 + uzc*dzt8

dvki1a = vxc*dxt1 + vyc*dyt1 + vzc*dzt1
dvki2a = vxc*dxt2 + vyc*dyt2 + vzc*dzt2
dvki3a = vxc*dxt3 + vyc*dyt3 + vzc*dzt3
dvki4a = vxc*dxt4 + vyc*dyt4 + vzc*dzt4
dvki5a = vxc*dxt5 + vyc*dyt5 + vzc*dzt5
dvki6a = vxc*dxt6 + vyc*dyt6 + vzc*dzt6
dvki7a = vxc*dxt7 + vyc*dyt7 + vzc*dzt7
dvki8a = vxc*dxt8 + vyc*dyt8 + vzc*dzt8

dwki1a = wxc*dxt1 + wyc*dyt1 + wzc*dzt1
dwki2a = wxc*dxt2 + wyc*dyt2 + wzc*dzt2
dwki3a = wxc*dxt3 + wyc*dyt3 + wzc*dzt3
dwki4a = wxc*dxt4 + wyc*dyt4 + wzc*dzt4
dwki5a = wxc*dxt5 + wyc*dyt5 + wzc*dzt5
dwki6a = wxc*dxt6 + wyc*dyt6 + wzc*dzt6
dwki7a = wxc*dxt7 + wyc*dyt7 + wzc*dzt7
dwki8a = wxc*dxt8 + wyc*dyt8 + wzc*dzt8

duki1b = uxc2*dxt1 + uyc2*dyt1 + uzc2*dzt1
duki2b = uxc2*dxt2 + uyc2*dyt2 + uzc2*dzt2
duki3b = uxc2*dxt3 + uyc2*dyt3 + uzc2*dzt3
duki4b = uxc2*dxt4 + uyc2*dyt4 + uzc2*dzt4
duki5b = uxc2*dxt5 + uyc2*dyt5 + uzc2*dzt5
duki6b = uxc2*dxt6 + uyc2*dyt6 + uzc2*dzt6
duki7b = uxc2*dxt7 + uyc2*dyt7 + uzc2*dzt7
duki8b = uxc2*dxt8 + uyc2*dyt8 + uzc2*dzt8

dvki1b = vxc2*dxt1 + vyc2*dyt1 + vzc2*dzt1
dvki2b = vxc2*dxt2 + vyc2*dyt2 + vzc2*dzt2
dvki3b = vxc2*dxt3 + vyc2*dyt3 + vzc2*dzt3
dvki4b = vxc2*dxt4 + vyc2*dyt4 + vzc2*dzt4
dvki5b = vxc2*dxt5 + vyc2*dyt5 + vzc2*dzt5
```

```
dvki6b = vxc2*dxt6 + vyc2*dyt6 + vzc2*dzt6
dvki7b = vxc2*dxt7 + vyc2*dyt7 + vzc2*dzt7
dvki8b = vxc2*dxt8 + vyc2*dyt8 + vzc2*dzt8

dwki1b = wxc2*dxt1 + wyc2*dyt1 + wzc2*dzt1
dwki2b = wxc2*dxt2 + wyc2*dyt2 + wzc2*dzt2
dwki3b = wxc2*dxt3 + wyc2*dyt3 + wzc2*dzt3
dwki4b = wxc2*dxt4 + wyc2*dyt4 + wzc2*dzt4
dwki5b = wxc2*dxt5 + wyc2*dyt5 + wzc2*dzt5
dwki6b = wxc2*dxt6 + wyc2*dyt6 + wzc2*dzt6
dwki7b = wxc2*dxt7 + wyc2*dyt7 + wzc2*dzt7
dwki8b = wxc2*dxt8 + wyc2*dyt8 + wzc2*dzt8

duki1c = uxc3*dxt1 + uyc3*dyt1 + uzc3*dzt1
duki2c = uxc3*dxt2 + uyc3*dyt2 + uzc3*dzt2
duki3c = uxc3*dxt3 + uyc3*dyt3 + uzc3*dzt3
duki4c = uxc3*dxt4 + uyc3*dyt4 + uzc3*dzt4
duki5c = uxc3*dxt5 + uyc3*dyt5 + uzc3*dzt5
duki6c = uxc3*dxt6 + uyc3*dyt6 + uzc3*dzt6
duki7c = uxc3*dxt7 + uyc3*dyt7 + uzc3*dzt7
duki8c = uxc3*dxt8 + uyc3*dyt8 + uzc3*dzt8

dvki1c = vxc3*dxt1 + vyc3*dyt1 + vzc3*dzt1
dvki2c = vxc3*dxt2 + vyc3*dyt2 + vzc3*dzt2
dvki3c = vxc3*dxt3 + vyc3*dyt3 + vzc3*dzt3
dvki4c = vxc3*dxt4 + vyc3*dyt4 + vzc3*dzt4
dvki5c = vxc3*dxt5 + vyc3*dyt5 + vzc3*dzt5
dvki6c = vxc3*dxt6 + vyc3*dyt6 + vzc3*dzt6
dvki7c = vxc3*dxt7 + vyc3*dyt7 + vzc3*dzt7
dvki8c = vxc3*dxt8 + vyc3*dyt8 + vzc3*dzt8

dwki1c = wxc3*dxt1 + wyc3*dyt1 + wzc3*dzt1
dwki2c = wxc3*dxt2 + wyc3*dyt2 + wzc3*dzt2
dwki3c = wxc3*dxt3 + wyc3*dyt3 + wzc3*dzt3
dwki4c = wxc3*dxt4 + wyc3*dyt4 + wzc3*dzt4
dwki5c = wxc3*dxt5 + wyc3*dyt5 + wzc3*dzt5
dwki6c = wxc3*dxt6 + wyc3*dyt6 + wzc3*dzt6
dwki7c = wxc3*dxt7 + wyc3*dyt7 + wzc3*dzt7
dwki8c = wxc3*dxt8 + wyc3*dyt8 + wzc3*dzt8

duki1d = uxc4*dxt1 + uyc4*dyt1 + uzc4*dzt1
duki2d = uxc4*dxt2 + uyc4*dyt2 + uzc4*dzt2
duki3d = uxc4*dxt3 + uyc4*dyt3 + uzc4*dzt3
```

```
duki4d = uxc4*dxt4 + uyc4*dyt4 + uzc4*dzt4
duki5d = uxc4*dxt5 + uyc4*dyt5 + uzc4*dzt5
duki6d = uxc4*dxt6 + uyc4*dyt6 + uzc4*dzt6
duki7d = uxc4*dxt7 + uyc4*dyt7 + uzc4*dzt7
duki8d = uxc4*dxt8 + uyc4*dyt8 + uzc4*dzt8

dvki1d = vxc4*dxt1 + vyc4*dyt1 + vzc4*dzt1
dvki2d = vxc4*dxt2 + vyc4*dyt2 + vzc4*dzt2
dvki3d = vxc4*dxt3 + vyc4*dyt3 + vzc4*dzt3
dvki4d = vxc4*dxt4 + vyc4*dyt4 + vzc4*dzt4
dvki5d = vxc4*dxt5 + vyc4*dyt5 + vzc4*dzt5
dvki6d = vxc4*dxt6 + vyc4*dyt6 + vzc4*dzt6
dvki7d = vxc4*dxt7 + vyc4*dyt7 + vzc4*dzt7
dvki8d = vxc4*dxt8 + vyc4*dyt8 + vzc4*dzt8

dwki1d = wxc4*dxt1 + wyc4*dyt1 + wzc4*dzt1
dwki2d = wxc4*dxt2 + wyc4*dyt2 + wzc4*dzt2
dwki3d = wxc4*dxt3 + wyc4*dyt3 + wzc4*dzt3
dwki4d = wxc4*dxt4 + wyc4*dyt4 + wzc4*dzt4
dwki5d = wxc4*dxt5 + wyc4*dyt5 + wzc4*dzt5
dwki6d = wxc4*dxt6 + wyc4*dyt6 + wzc4*dzt6
dwki7d = wxc4*dxt7 + wyc4*dyt7 + wzc4*dzt7
dwki8d = wxc4*dxt8 + wyc4*dyt8 + wzc4*dzt8

! Finish with image coordinates themselves:
fac1 = -fc/wki
fac2 = fc*uki/wki**2
duda(1) = fac1*duki1a + fac2*dwki1a
duda(2) = fac1*duki2a + fac2*dwki2a
duda(3) = fac1*duki3a + fac2*dwki3a
duda(4) = fac1*duki4a + fac2*dwki4a
duda(5) = fac1*duki5a + fac2*dwki5a
duda(6) = fac1*duki6a + fac2*dwki6a
duda(7) = fac1*duki7a + fac2*dwki7a
duda(8) = fac1*duki8a + fac2*dwki8a

fac2 = fc*vki/wki**2
dvda(1) = fac1*dvki1a + fac2*dwki1a
dvda(2) = fac1*dvki2a + fac2*dwki2a
dvda(3) = fac1*dvki3a + fac2*dwki3a
dvda(4) = fac1*dvki4a + fac2*dwki4a
dvda(5) = fac1*dvki5a + fac2*dwki5a
dvda(6) = fac1*dvki6a + fac2*dwki6a
```

```
dvda(7) = fac1*dvki7a + fac2*dwki7a
dvda(8) = fac1*dvki8a + fac2*dwki8a

fac3 = -fc/wki2
fac4 = fc*uki2/wki2**2
duda2(1) = fac3*duki1b + fac4*dwki1b
duda2(2) = fac3*duki2b + fac4*dwki2b
duda2(3) = fac3*duki3b + fac4*dwki3b
duda2(4) = fac3*duki4b + fac4*dwki4b
duda2(5) = fac3*duki5b + fac4*dwki5b
duda2(6) = fac3*duki6b + fac4*dwki6b
duda2(7) = fac3*duki7b + fac4*dwki7b
duda2(8) = fac3*duki8b + fac4*dwki8b

fac4 = fc*vki2/wki2**2
dvda2(1) = fac3*dvki1b + fac4*dwki1b
dvda2(2) = fac3*dvki2b + fac4*dwki2b
dvda2(3) = fac3*dvki3b + fac4*dwki3b
dvda2(4) = fac3*dvki4b + fac4*dwki4b
dvda2(5) = fac3*dvki5b + fac4*dwki5b
dvda2(6) = fac3*dvki6b + fac4*dwki6b
dvda2(7) = fac3*dvki7b + fac4*dwki7b
dvda2(8) = fac3*dvki8b + fac4*dwki8b

fac5 = -fc/wki3
fac6 = fc*uki3/wki3**2
duda3(1) = fac5*duki1c + fac6*dwki1c
duda3(2) = fac5*duki2c + fac6*dwki2c
duda3(3) = fac5*duki3c + fac6*dwki3c
duda3(4) = fac5*duki4c + fac6*dwki4c
duda3(5) = fac5*duki5c + fac6*dwki5c
duda3(6) = fac5*duki6c + fac6*dwki6c
duda3(7) = fac5*duki7c + fac6*dwki7c
duda3(8) = fac5*duki8c + fac6*dwki8c

fac6 = fc*vki3/wki3**2
dvda3(1) = fac5*dvki1c + fac6*dwki1c
dvda3(2) = fac5*dvki2c + fac6*dwki2c
dvda3(3) = fac5*dvki3c + fac6*dwki3c
dvda3(4) = fac5*dvki4c + fac6*dwki4c
dvda3(5) = fac5*dvki5c + fac6*dwki5c
dvda3(6) = fac5*dvki6c + fac6*dwki6c
dvda3(7) = fac5*dvki7c + fac6*dwki7c
```

```
            dvda3(8) = fac5*dvki8c + fac6*dwki8c


            fac7 = -fc/wki4
            fac8 = fc*uki4/wki2**2
            duda4(1) = fac7*duki1d + fac8*dwki1d
            duda4(2) = fac7*duki2d + fac8*dwki2d
            duda4(3) = fac7*duki3d + fac8*dwki3d
            duda4(4) = fac7*duki4d + fac8*dwki4d
            duda4(5) = fac7*duki5d + fac8*dwki5d
            duda4(6) = fac7*duki6d + fac8*dwki6d
            duda4(7) = fac7*duki7d + fac8*dwki7d
            duda4(8) = fac7*duki8d + fac8*dwki8d

            fac8 = fc*vki4/wki4**2
            dvda4(1) = fac7*dvki1d + fac8*dwki1d
            dvda4(2) = fac7*dvki2d + fac8*dwki2d
            dvda4(3) = fac7*dvki3d + fac8*dwki3d
            dvda4(4) = fac7*dvki4d + fac8*dwki4d
            dvda4(5) = fac7*dvki5d + fac8*dwki5d
            dvda4(6) = fac7*dvki6d + fac8*dwki6d
            dvda4(7) = fac7*dvki7d + fac8*dwki7d
            dvda4(8) = fac7*dvki8d + fac8*dwki8d

            end

ccccccccccccccccccccccccccccccccccccccccccccccccccccccccccccc

            FUNCTION gasdev(idum)
            INTEGER idum
            REAL gasdev
CU          USES ran1
            INTEGER iset
            REAL fac,gset,rsq,v1,v2,ran1
            SAVE iset,gset
            DATA iset/0/
            if (iset.eq.0) then
1             v1=2.*ran1(idum)-1.
              v2=2.*ran1(idum)-1.
              rsq=v1**2+v2**2
              if(rsq.ge.1..or.rsq.eq.0.)goto 1
              fac=sqrt(-2.*log(rsq)/rsq)
              gset=v1*fac
              gasdev=v2*fac
```

```
      iset=1
    else
      gasdev=gset
      iset=0
    endif
    return
    END
C  (C) Copr. 1986-92 Numerical Recipes Software ~-259u..
```

ccccccccccccccccccccccccccccccccccccccccccccccccccccccccc

```
      FUNCTION ran1(idum)
      INTEGER idum,IA,IM,IQ,IR,NTAB,NDIV
      REAL ran1,AM,EPS,RNMX
      PARAMETER (IA=16807,IM=2147483647,AM=1./IM,IQ=127773,IR=2836,
     *NTAB=32,NDIV=1+(IM-1)/NTAB,EPS=1.2e-7,RNMX=1.-EPS)
      INTEGER j,k,iv(NTAB),iy
      SAVE iv,iy
      DATA iv /NTAB*0/, iy /0/
      if (idum.le.0.or.iy.eq.0) then
        idum=max(-idum,1)
        do 11 j=NTAB+8,1,-1
          k=idum/IQ
          idum=IA*(idum-k*IQ)-IR*k
          if (idum.lt.0) idum=idum+IM
          if (j.le.NTAB) iv(j)=idum
11      continue
        iy=iv(1)
      endif
      k=idum/IQ
      idum=IA*(idum-k*IQ)-IR*k
      if (idum.lt.0) idum=idum+IM
      j=1+iy/NDIV
      iy=iv(j)
      iv(j)=idum
      ran1=min(AM*iy,RNMX)
      return
      END
C  (C) Copr. 1986-92 Numerical Recipes Software ~-259u..
```

ccccccccccccccccccccccccccccccccccccccccccccccccccccccccc

```
      SUBROUTINE choldc(a,n,np,p,ierr)
```

```fortran
      INTEGER n,np
      real a(np,np),p(n)
      INTEGER i,j,k
      real sum
      ierr=0
      do 13 i=1,n
        do 12 j=i,n
          sum=a(i,j)
          do 11 k=i-1,1,-1
            sum=sum-a(i,k)*a(j,k)
11        continue
          if(i.eq.j)then
            if(sum.le.0.)then
              ierr=i
              return
            endif
            p(i)=sqrt(sum)
          else
            a(j,i)=sum/p(i)
          endif
12      continue
13    continue
      return
      END
C  (C) Copr. 1986-92 Numerical Recipes Software ~-259u..
```

ccccccccccccccccccccccccccccccccccccccccccccccccccccccccc

```fortran
      SUBROUTINE cholsl(a,n,np,p,b,x)
      INTEGER n,np
      real a(np,np),b(n),p(n),x(n)
      INTEGER i,k
      real sum
      do 12 i=1,n
        sum=b(i)
        do 11 k=i-1,1,-1
          sum=sum-a(i,k)*x(k)
11      continue
        x(i)=sum/p(i)
12    continue
      do 14 i=n,1,-1
        sum=x(i)
        do 13 k=i+1,n
          sum=sum-a(k,i)*x(k)
```

```
13      continue
        x(i)=sum/p(i)
14    continue
      return
      END
C  (C) Copr. 1986-92 Numerical Recipes Software ~-259u..
```

ccccccccccccccccccccccccccccccccccccccccccccccccccccccc

Appendix C. Data Runs

C.1 Runs Varying Number of Data Points

BC=.7, TC=.1, XDF=2, YDF=1

	FIT	EXACT	ERROR	PRECISION
DeltaX_k:	5.04862	5.00000	0.04862	0.03647
DeltaY_k:	-0.01996	0.00000	-0.01996	0.00680
DeltaZ_k:	-19.80795	-20.00000	0.19205	0.13681
Alpha_k:	14.99984	15.00000	-0.00016	0.09458
Beta_k:	9.99999	10.00000	-0.00001	0.04803
Phi_k:	-0.70264	5.00000	-5.70264	4.03329
BC:	0.01686	0.70000	-0.68314	0.47691
TC:	0.10088	0.10000	0.00088	0.00578

BC=.7, TC=.1, XDF=2, YDF=2

	FIT	EXACT	ERROR	PRECISION
DeltaX_k:	5.00349	5.00000	0.00349	0.00876
DeltaY_k:	-0.02274	0.00000	-0.02274	0.00825
DeltaZ_k:	-19.98313	-20.00000	0.01687	0.02371
Alpha_k:	14.98879	15.00000	-0.01121	0.13638
Beta_k:	9.97992	10.00000	-0.02008	0.07218
Phi_k:	4.52164	5.00000	-0.47836	0.37489
BC:	0.63206	0.70000	-0.06794	0.04131
TC:	0.09930	0.10000	-0.00070	0.00805

BC=.7, TC=.1, XDF=3, YDF=3

	FIT	EXACT	ERROR	PRECISION
DeltaX_k:	5.00374	5.00000	0.00374	0.00579
DeltaY_k:	-0.02149	0.00000	-0.02149	0.00521
DeltaZ_k:	-19.98270	-20.00000	0.01730	0.01614
Alpha_k:	14.98958	15.00000	-0.01042	0.09566
Beta_k:	9.97997	10.00000	-0.02003	0.04839
Phi_k:	4.55500	5.00000	-0.44500	0.23367
BC:	0.63709	0.70000	-0.06291	0.02502
TC:	0.09932	0.10000	-0.00068	0.00565

BC=.7, TC=.1, XDF=4, YDF=4

	FIT	EXACT	ERROR	PRECISION
DeltaX_k:	5.00419	5.00000	0.00419	0.00446
DeltaY_k:	-0.02088	0.00000	-0.02088	0.00387
DeltaZ_k:	-19.98127	-20.00000	0.01873	0.01275
Alpha_k:	14.99018	15.00000	-0.00982	0.07570

	FIT	EXACT	ERROR	PRECISION
Beta_k:	9.97992	10.00000	-0.02008	0.03721
Phi_k:	4.54965	5.00000	-0.45035	0.17845
BC:	0.63745	0.70000	-0.06255	0.01877
TC:	0.09935	0.10000	-0.00065	0.00446

BC=.7, TC=.1, XDF=5, YDF=5

	FIT	EXACT	ERROR	PRECISION
DeltaX_k:	5.00463	5.00000	0.00463	0.00367
DeltaY_k:	-0.02054	0.00000	-0.02054	0.00310
DeltaZ_k:	-19.97978	-20.00000	0.02022	0.01069
Alpha_k:	14.99060	15.00000	-0.00940	0.06315
Beta_k:	9.97989	10.00000	-0.02011	0.03044
Phi_k:	4.53620	5.00000	-0.46380	0.14722
BC:	0.63671	0.70000	-0.06329	0.01529
TC:	0.09938	0.10000	-0.00062	0.00372

BC=.7, TC=.1, XDF=6, YDF=6

	FIT	EXACT	ERROR	PRECISION
DeltaX_k:	5.00502	5.00000	0.00502	0.00313
DeltaY_k:	-0.02033	0.00000	-0.02033	0.00260
DeltaZ_k:	-19.97836	-20.00000	0.02164	0.00927
Alpha_k:	14.99095	15.00000	-0.00905	0.05434
Beta_k:	9.97990	10.00000	-0.02010	0.02582
Phi_k:	4.52055	5.00000	-0.47945	0.12648
BC:	0.63559	0.70000	-0.06441	0.01302
TC:	0.09940	0.10000	-0.00060	0.00320

BC=.4, TC=.01, XDF=2, YDF=1

	FIT	EXACT	ERROR	PRECISION
DeltaX_k:	5.02026	5.00000	0.02026	0.01264
DeltaY_k:	-0.01066	0.00000	-0.01066	0.00329
DeltaZ_k:	-19.91855	-20.00000	0.08145	0.04907
Alpha_k:	15.00007	15.00000	0.00007	0.02811
Beta_k:	10.00007	10.00000	0.00007	0.01437
Phi_k:	2.57657	5.00000	-2.42343	1.44473
BC:	0.11146	0.40000	-0.28854	0.17059
TC:	0.01003	0.01000	0.00003	0.00167

BC=.4, TC=.01, XDF=2, YDF=2

	FIT	EXACT	ERROR	PRECISION
DeltaX_k:	5.00064	5.00000	0.00064	0.00305
DeltaY_k:	-0.00792	0.00000	-0.00792	0.00290
DeltaZ_k:	-19.99675	-20.00000	0.00325	0.00833

	FIT	EXACT	ERROR	PRECISION
Alpha_k:	14.99670	15.00000	-0.00330	0.04744
Beta_k:	9.99206	10.00000	-0.00794	0.02509
Phi_k:	4.89159	5.00000	-0.10841	0.13443
BC:	0.38430	0.40000	-0.01570	0.01491
TC:	0.00993	0.01000	-0.00007	0.00282

BC=.4, TC=.01, XDF=3, YDF=3

	FIT	EXACT	ERROR	PRECISION
DeltaX_k:	5.00072	5.00000	0.00072	0.00202
DeltaY_k:	-0.00743	0.00000	-0.00743	0.00183
DeltaZ_k:	-19.99668	-20.00000	0.00332	0.00564
Alpha_k:	14.99698	15.00000	-0.00302	0.03315
Beta_k:	9.99198	10.00000	-0.00802	0.01675
Phi_k:	4.90041	5.00000	-0.09959	0.08324
BC:	0.38556	0.40000	-0.01444	0.00898
TC:	0.00994	0.01000	-0.00006	0.00197

BC=.4, TC=.01, XDF=4, YDF=4

	FIT	EXACT	ERROR	PRECISION
DeltaX_k:	5.00084	5.00000	0.00084	0.00156
DeltaY_k:	-0.00722	0.00000	-0.00722	0.00136
DeltaZ_k:	-19.99636	-20.00000	0.00364	0.00445
Alpha_k:	14.99715	15.00000	-0.00285	0.02624
Beta_k:	9.99185	10.00000	-0.00815	0.01288
Phi_k:	4.89945	5.00000	-0.10055	0.06357
BC:	0.38565	0.40000	-0.01435	0.00674
TC:	0.00994	0.01000	-0.00006	0.00156

BC=.4, TC=.01, XDF=5, YDF=5

	FIT	EXACT	ERROR	PRECISION
DeltaX_k:	5.00095	5.00000	0.00095	0.00128
DeltaY_k:	-0.00710	0.00000	-0.00710	0.00110
DeltaZ_k:	-19.99602	-20.00000	0.00398	0.00374
Alpha_k:	14.99725	15.00000	-0.00275	0.02191
Beta_k:	9.99174	10.00000	-0.00826	0.01054
Phi_k:	4.89640	5.00000	-0.10360	0.05254
BC:	0.38547	0.40000	-0.01453	0.00550
TC:	0.00994	0.01000	-0.00006	0.00130

C.2 Runs Varying Number of Cameras

BC= .4, TC= .01, Cameras= 1

	FIT	EXACT	ERROR	PRECISION

	FIT	EXACT	ERROR	PRECISION
DeltaX_k:	4.99583	5.00000	-0.00417	0.00079
DeltaY_k:	0.00003	0.00000	0.00003	0.00064
DeltaZ_k:	-19.98162	-20.00000	0.01838	0.00253
Alpha_k:	14.85465	15.00000	-0.14535	0.01806
Beta_k:	9.97567	10.00000	-0.02433	0.00436
Phi_k:	4.86896	5.00000	-0.13104	0.03536
BC:	0.37456	0.40000	-0.02544	0.00392
TC:	0.00753	0.01000	-0.00247	0.00087

BC= .4, TC= .01, Cameras= 1 and 2

	FIT	EXACT	ERROR	PRECISION
DeltaX_k:	5.00255	5.00000	0.00255	0.00109
DeltaY_k:	-0.00559	0.00000	-0.00559	0.00079
DeltaZ_k:	-19.98990	-20.00000	0.01010	0.00390
Alpha_k:	14.99461	15.00000	-0.00539	0.02109
Beta_k:	9.98918	10.00000	-0.01082	0.00870
Phi_k:	4.79492	5.00000	-0.20508	0.06247
BC:	0.37142	0.40000	-0.02858	0.00744
TC:	0.00885	0.01000	-0.00115	0.00158

BC= .4, TC= .01, Cameras= 1 and 3

	FIT	EXACT	ERROR	PRECISION
DeltaX_k:	5.00062	5.00000	0.00062	0.00068
DeltaY_k:	-0.00421	0.00000	-0.00421	0.00065
DeltaZ_k:	-19.99755	-20.00000	0.00245	0.00209
Alpha_k:	14.99545	15.00000	-0.00455	0.01065
Beta_k:	9.99457	10.00000	-0.00543	0.00605
Phi_k:	4.92415	5.00000	-0.07585	0.03221
BC:	0.38603	0.40000	-0.01397	0.00372
TC:	0.00882	0.01000	-0.00118	0.00072

BC= .4, TC= .01, Cameras= 1 and 4

	FIT	EXACT	ERROR	PRECISION
DeltaX_k:	5.00182	5.00000	0.00182	0.00068
DeltaY_k:	-0.00508	0.00000	-0.00508	0.00057
DeltaZ_k:	-19.99741	-20.00000	0.00259	0.00263
Alpha_k:	14.98318	15.00000	-0.01682	0.01416
Beta_k:	9.97089	10.00000	-0.02911	0.00535
Phi_k:	4.86932	5.00000	-0.13068	0.04006
BC:	0.36655	0.40000	-0.03345	0.00452
TC:	0.00986	0.01000	-0.00014	0.00098

BC= .4, TC= .01, Cameras= 4

	FIT	EXACT	ERROR	PRECISION
DeltaX_k:	5.00081	5.00000	0.00081	0.00078
DeltaY_k:	-0.00472	0.00000	-0.00472	0.00069
DeltaZ_k:	-19.99675	-20.00000	0.00325	0.00245
Alpha_k:	14.99423	15.00000	-0.00577	0.01243
Beta_k:	9.99360	10.00000	-0.00641	0.00671
Phi_k:	4.90767	5.00000	-0.09233	0.03790
BC:	0.38420	0.40000	-0.01580	0.00444
TC:	0.00876	0.01000	-0.00124	0.00087

BC= .4, TC= .01, Cameras= 8

	FIT	EXACT	ERROR	PRECISION
DeltaX_k:	5.00081	5.00000	0.00081	0.00078
DeltaY_k:	-0.00472	0.00000	-0.00472	0.00069
DeltaZ_k:	-19.99675	-20.00000	0.00325	0.00245
Alpha_k:	14.99423	15.00000	-0.00577	0.01243
Beta_k:	9.99360	10.00000	-0.00641	0.00671
Phi_k:	4.90767	5.00000	-0.09233	0.03790
BC:	0.38420	0.40000	-0.01580	0.00444
TC:	0.00876	0.01000	-0.00124	0.00087

BC= 1, TC= .5, Cameras= 1

	FIT	EXACT	ERROR	PRECISION
DeltaX_k:	1.39916	5.00000	-3.60084	1.72027
DeltaY_k:	2.34957	0.00000	2.34957	1.25111
DeltaZ_k:	-3.32290	-20.00000	16.67710	7.50294
Alpha_k:	-8.38708	15.00000	-23.38708	14.45716
Beta_k:	2.17753	10.00000	-7.82247	7.62531
Phi_k:	-4.85253	5.00000	-9.85253	24.85895
BC:	-9.75151	1.00000	-10.75151	31.04010
TC:	4.70599	0.50000	4.20599	17.06678

BC= 1, TC= .5, Cameras= 1 and 2

	FIT	EXACT	ERROR	PRECISION
DeltaX_k:	5.01123	5.00000	0.01123	0.00536
DeltaY_k:	-0.01977	0.00000	-0.01977	0.00437
DeltaZ_k:	-19.92888	-20.00000	0.07112	0.01960
Alpha_k:	14.77107	15.00000	-0.22893	0.11429
Beta_k:	10.03690	10.00000	0.03690	0.05043
Phi_k:	3.12636	5.00000	-1.87364	0.29504
BC:	0.67148	1.00000	-0.32852	0.03427
TC:	0.43699	0.50000	-0.06301	0.00805

BC= 1, TC= .5, Cameras= 1 and 3

	FIT	EXACT	ERROR	PRECISION
DeltaX_k:	5.00420	5.00000	0.00420	0.00449
DeltaY_k:	-0.02007	0.00000	-0.02007	0.00436
DeltaZ_k:	-19.97640	-20.00000	0.02360	0.01420
Alpha_k:	14.75491	15.00000	-0.24509	0.07321
Beta_k:	9.99202	10.00000	-0.00798	0.04222
Phi_k:	3.82213	5.00000	-1.17787	0.21012
BC:	0.73340	1.00000	-0.26660	0.02385
TC:	0.43463	0.50000	-0.06537	0.00484

BC= 1, TC= .5, Cameras= 1 and 4

	FIT	EXACT	ERROR	PRECISION
DeltaX_k:	5.00966	5.00000	0.00966	0.00412
DeltaY_k:	-0.02296	0.00000	-0.02296	0.00360
DeltaZ_k:	-19.97364	-20.00000	0.02636	0.01743
Alpha_k:	14.71916	15.00000	-0.28084	0.09659
Beta_k:	9.88608	10.00000	-0.11392	0.03871
Phi_k:	3.60765	5.00000	-1.39235	0.24747
BC:	0.64836	1.00000	-0.35164	0.02631
TC:	0.45221	0.50000	-0.04779	0.00632

BC= 1, TC= .5, Cameras= 4

	FIT	EXACT	ERROR	PRECISION
DeltaX_k:	5.00494	5.00000	0.00494	0.00476
DeltaY_k:	-0.02169	0.00000	-0.02169	0.00432
DeltaZ_k:	-19.97067	-20.00000	0.02933	0.01524
Alpha_k:	14.77376	15.00000	-0.22624	0.07916
Beta_k:	9.99640	10.00000	-0.00360	0.04367
Phi_k:	3.74769	5.00000	-1.25231	0.22587
BC:	0.72692	1.00000	-0.27308	0.02606
TC:	0.43588	0.50000	-0.06412	0.00549

BC= 1, TC= .5, Cameras= 8

	FIT	EXACT	ERROR	PRECISION
DeltaX_k:	5.00494	5.00000	0.00494	0.00476
DeltaY_k:	-0.02169	0.00000	-0.02169	0.00432
DeltaZ_k:	-19.97067	-20.00000	0.02933	0.01524
Alpha_k:	14.77376	15.00000	-0.22624	0.07916
Beta_k:	9.99640	10.00000	-0.00360	0.04367
Phi_k:	3.74769	5.00000	-1.25231	0.22587
BC:	0.72692	1.00000	-0.27308	0.02606
TC:	0.43588	0.50000	-0.06412	0.00549

C.3 Runs Varying Bending Coefficient

BC= .01, Deformation Model

	FIT	EXACT	ERROR	PRECISION
DeltaX_k:	5.00000	5.00000	0.00000	0.00000
DeltaY_k:	0.00000	0.00000	0.00000	0.00000
DeltaZ_k:	-20.00000	-20.00000	0.00000	0.00000
Alpha_k:	14.99999	15.00000	-0.00001	0.00001
Beta_k:	10.00000	10.00000	0.00000	0.00001
Phi_k:	4.99998	5.00000	-0.00002	0.00003
BC:	0.01000	0.01000	0.00000	0.00000
TC:	0.00000	0.00000	0.00000	0.00000

BC= .01, Rigid Model

	FIT	EXACT	ERROR	PRECISION
DeltaX_k:	5.00106	5.00000	0.00106	0.00024
DeltaY_k:	-0.00059	0.00000	-0.00059	0.00068
DeltaZ_k:	-19.99575	-20.00000	0.00425	0.00033
Alpha_k:	14.99992	15.00000	-0.00008	0.00227
Beta_k:	9.99988	10.00000	-0.00012	0.00232
Phi_k:	4.91773	5.00000	-0.08227	0.00253

BC= .1, Deformation Model

	FIT	EXACT	ERROR	PRECISION
DeltaX_k:	5.00001	5.00000	0.00001	0.00005
DeltaY_k:	-0.00029	0.00000	-0.00029	0.00005
DeltaZ_k:	-19.99997	-20.00000	0.00003	0.00016
Alpha_k:	14.99990	15.00000	-0.00010	0.00080
Beta_k:	9.99954	10.00000	-0.00046	0.00043
Phi_k:	4.99824	5.00000	-0.00176	0.00248
BC:	0.09966	0.10000	-0.00034	0.00029
TC:	0.00000	0.00000	0.00000	0.00006

BC= .1, Rigid Model

	FIT	EXACT	ERROR	PRECISION
DeltaX_k:	5.01069	5.00000	0.01069	0.00245
DeltaY_k:	-0.00552	0.00000	-0.00552	0.00684
DeltaZ_k:	-19.95743	-20.00000	0.04257	0.00328
Alpha_k:	14.99931	15.00000	-0.00069	0.02273
Beta_k:	9.99917	10.00000	-0.00083	0.02322
Phi_k:	4.17712	5.00000	-0.82288	0.02531

BC= .5, Deformation Model

	FIT	EXACT	ERROR	PRECISION

	FIT	EXACT	ERROR	PRECISION
DeltaX_k:	5.00164	5.00000	0.00164	0.00121
DeltaY_k:	-0.00741	0.00000	-0.00741	0.00106
DeltaZ_k:	-19.99336	-20.00000	0.00664	0.00376
Alpha_k:	14.99815	15.00000	-0.00185	0.01917
Beta_k:	9.98995	10.00000	-0.01005	0.01033
Phi_k:	4.84557	5.00000	-0.15443	0.05792
BC:	0.47671	0.50000	-0.02329	0.00678
TC:	0.00004	0.00000	0.00004	0.00135

BC= .5, Rigid Model

	FIT	EXACT	ERROR	PRECISION
DeltaX_k:	5.05461	5.00000	0.05461	0.01214
DeltaY_k:	-0.01835	0.00000	-0.01835	0.03389
DeltaZ_k:	-19.78743	-20.00000	0.21257	0.01624
Alpha_k:	14.99723	15.00000	-0.00277	0.11302
Beta_k:	10.00333	10.00000	0.00333	0.11497
Phi_k:	0.89955	5.00000	-4.10045	0.12528

BC= 1, Deformation Model

	FIT	EXACT	ERROR	PRECISION
DeltaX_k:	5.01074	5.00000	0.01074	0.00429
DeltaY_k:	-0.02702	0.00000	-0.02702	0.00370
DeltaZ_k:	-19.95592	-20.00000	0.04408	0.01306
Alpha_k:	14.99634	15.00000	-0.00366	0.06861
Beta_k:	9.96896	10.00000	-0.03104	0.03708
Phi_k:	4.06393	5.00000	-0.93607	0.19693
BC:	0.86144	1.00000	-0.13856	0.02288
TC:	0.00033	0.00000	0.00033	0.00478

BC= 1, Rigid Model

	FIT	EXACT	ERROR	PRECISION
DeltaX_k:	5.11041	5.00000	0.11041	0.02349
DeltaY_k:	-0.01434	0.00000	-0.01434	0.06557
DeltaZ_k:	-19.58135	-20.00000	0.41865	0.03144
Alpha_k:	14.99623	15.00000	-0.00377	0.21994
Beta_k:	10.02420	10.00000	0.02420	0.22432
Phi_k:	-3.08916	5.00000	-8.08916	0.24509

BC= 3, Deformation Model

	FIT	EXACT	ERROR	PRECISION
DeltaX_k:	5.10721	5.00000	0.10721	0.02075
DeltaY_k:	-0.09868	0.00000	-0.09868	0.02103
DeltaZ_k:	-19.57897	-20.00000	0.42103	0.05638

```
Alpha_k:   15.00817   15.00000    0.00817   0.32444
 Beta_k:    9.91008   10.00000   -0.08992   0.19254
  Phi_k:   -3.63004    5.00000   -8.63004   0.81679
     BC:    1.56135    3.00000   -1.43865   0.09315
     TC:    0.00268    0.00000    0.00268   0.02301
```

BC= 3, Rigid Model

```
              FIT       EXACT      ERROR    PRECISION
DeltaX_k:    5.30461    5.00000    0.30461   0.05296
DeltaY_k:    0.14225    0.00000    0.14225   0.14660
DeltaZ_k:  -18.93527  -20.00000    1.06473   0.07232
 Alpha_k:   15.00500   15.00000    0.00500   0.51051
  Beta_k:   10.21304   10.00000    0.21304   0.55756
   Phi_k:  -16.40640    5.00000  -21.40640   0.62795
```

C.4   Runs Varying Twisting Coefficient

TC= .01, Deformation Model

```
              FIT       EXACT      ERROR    PRECISION
DeltaX_k:    4.99998    5.00000   -0.00002   0.00005
DeltaY_k:    0.00001    0.00000    0.00001   0.00005
DeltaZ_k:  -20.00007  -20.00000   -0.00007   0.00017
 Alpha_k:   14.99562   15.00000   -0.00438   0.00085
  Beta_k:   10.00040   10.00000    0.00040   0.00046
   Phi_k:    4.98921    5.00000   -0.01079   0.00263
      BC:    0.00676    0.01000   -0.00324   0.00031
      TC:    0.00876    0.01000   -0.00124   0.00006
```

TC= .01, Rigid Model

```
              FIT       EXACT      ERROR    PRECISION
DeltaX_k:    4.99906    5.00000   -0.00094   0.00116
DeltaY_k:    0.00081    0.00000    0.00081   0.00325
DeltaZ_k:  -20.00455  -20.00000   -0.00455   0.00156
 Alpha_k:   14.91409   15.00000   -0.08591   0.01079
  Beta_k:   10.00640   10.00000    0.00641   0.01104
   Phi_k:    4.94461    5.00000   -0.05539   0.01204
```

TC= .05, Deformation Model

```
              FIT       EXACT      ERROR    PRECISION
DeltaX_k:    4.99991    5.00000   -0.00009   0.00027
DeltaY_k:    0.00006    0.00000    0.00006   0.00025
DeltaZ_k:  -20.00034  -20.00000   -0.00034   0.00084
 Alpha_k:   14.97813   15.00000   -0.02187   0.00424
```

	Beta_k:	10.00212	10.00000	0.00212	0.00230
	Phi_k:	4.94589	5.00000	-0.05411	0.01319
	BC:	-0.00621	0.01000	-0.01621	0.00156
	TC:	0.04382	0.05000	-0.00618	0.00030

TC= .05, Rigid Model

	FIT	EXACT	ERROR	PRECISION
DeltaX_k:	4.99128	5.00000	-0.00872	0.00569
DeltaY_k:	0.00694	0.00000	0.00694	0.01592
DeltaZ_k:	-20.03975	-20.00000	-0.03975	0.00765
Alpha_k:	14.57080	15.00000	-0.42920	0.05290
Beta_k:	10.03350	10.00000	0.03350	0.05403
Phi_k:	5.05175	5.00000	0.05175	0.05894

TC= .1, Deformation Model

	FIT	EXACT	ERROR	PRECISION
DeltaX_k:	4.99979	5.00000	-0.00021	0.00053
DeltaY_k:	0.00015	0.00000	0.00015	0.00049
DeltaZ_k:	-20.00066	-20.00000	-0.00066	0.00169
Alpha_k:	14.95634	15.00000	-0.04366	0.00848
Beta_k:	10.00447	10.00000	0.00447	0.00461
Phi_k:	4.89178	5.00000	-0.10822	0.02640
BC:	-0.02242	0.01000	-0.03242	0.00311
TC:	0.08765	0.10000	-0.01235	0.00060

TC= .1, Rigid Model

	FIT	EXACT	ERROR	PRECISION
DeltaX_k:	4.98203	5.00000	-0.01797	0.01136
DeltaY_k:	0.01575	0.00000	0.01575	0.03180
DeltaZ_k:	-20.08369	-20.00000	-0.08369	0.01531
Alpha_k:	14.14184	15.00000	-0.85816	0.10574
Beta_k:	10.06980	10.00000	0.06980	0.10778
Phi_k:	5.18478	5.00000	0.18478	0.11765

TC= .5, Deformation Model

	FIT	EXACT	ERROR	PRECISION
DeltaX_k:	4.99781	5.00000	-0.00219	0.00258
DeltaY_k:	0.00182	0.00000	0.00182	0.00245
DeltaZ_k:	-20.00473	-20.00000	-0.00473	0.00838
Alpha_k:	14.78735	15.00000	-0.21265	0.04266
Beta_k:	10.02972	10.00000	0.02972	0.02363
Phi_k:	4.49688	5.00000	-0.50312	0.12920
BC:	-0.14748	0.01000	-0.15748	0.01519

```
     TC:    0.43906    0.50000   -0.06094    0.00301
```

TC= .5, Rigid Model

	FIT	EXACT	ERROR	PRECISION
DeltaX_k:	4.92767	5.00000	-0.07233	0.05573
DeltaY_k:	0.13080	0.00000	0.13080	0.15758
DeltaZ_k:	-20.43194	-20.00000	-0.43194	0.07659
Alpha_k:	10.72178	15.00000	-4.27822	0.52660
Beta_k:	10.44790	10.00000	0.44790	0.52917
Phi_k:	6.21184	5.00000	1.21184	0.58048

TC= 1, Deformation Model

	FIT	EXACT	ERROR	PRECISION
DeltaX_k:	4.99227	5.00000	-0.00773	0.00497
DeltaY_k:	0.00623	0.00000	0.00623	0.00496
DeltaZ_k:	-20.01830	-20.00000	-0.01830	0.01592
Alpha_k:	14.60260	15.00000	-0.39740	0.08536
Beta_k:	10.06853	10.00000	0.06853	0.04955
Phi_k:	4.20049	5.00000	-0.79951	0.23804
BC:	-0.28052	0.01000	-0.29052	0.02802
TC:	0.88034	1.00000	-0.11966	0.00609

TC= 1, Rigid Model

	FIT	EXACT	ERROR	PRECISION
DeltaX_k:	4.90840	5.00000	-0.09160	0.10818
DeltaY_k:	0.38357	0.00000	0.38357	0.30818
DeltaZ_k:	-20.85516	-20.00000	-0.85516	0.15187
Alpha_k:	6.49211	15.00000	-8.50789	1.04132
Beta_k:	11.12772	10.00000	1.12772	1.03227
Phi_k:	7.40292	5.00000	2.40292	1.13983

TC= 2, Deformation Model

	FIT	EXACT	ERROR	PRECISION
DeltaX_k:	4.97704	5.00000	-0.02296	0.00966
DeltaY_k:	0.01739	0.00000	0.01739	0.01051
DeltaZ_k:	-20.06331	-20.00000	-0.06331	0.02724
Alpha_k:	14.37409	15.00000	-0.62592	0.16181
Beta_k:	10.13054	10.00000	0.13054	0.10814
Phi_k:	4.12335	5.00000	-0.87665	0.37434
BC:	-0.48618	0.01000	-0.49618	0.04486
TC:	1.76974	2.00000	-0.23026	0.01232

TC= 2, Rigid Model

	FIT	EXACT	ERROR	PRECISION
DeltaX_k:	5.02440	5.00000	0.02440	0.20041
DeltaY_k:	1.21371	0.00000	1.21371	0.56798
DeltaZ_k:	-21.63817	-20.00000	-1.63817	0.28936
Alpha_k:	-1.71328	15.00000	-16.71328	1.99238
Beta_k:	13.04812	10.00000	3.04812	1.94719
Phi_k:	9.47545	5.00000	4.47545	2.17946

C.5 Runs Varying Noise

Noise= .01, Deformation Model

	FIT	EXACT	ERROR	PRECISION
DeltaX_k:	5.00489	5.00000	0.00489	0.00477
DeltaY_k:	-0.02170	0.00000	-0.02170	0.00432
DeltaZ_k:	-19.97081	-20.00000	0.02919	0.01526
Alpha_k:	14.77310	15.00000	-0.22690	0.07927
Beta_k:	9.99619	10.00000	-0.00381	0.04373
Phi_k:	3.74983	5.00000	-1.25017	0.22617
BC:	0.72717	1.00000	-0.27283	0.02609
TC:	0.43586	0.50000	-0.06414	0.00549

Noise= .01, Rigid Model

	FIT	EXACT	ERROR	PRECISION
DeltaX_k:	5.01658	5.00000	0.01658	0.06005
DeltaY_k:	0.09526	0.00000	0.09526	0.16851
DeltaZ_k:	-20.01979	-20.00000	-0.01979	0.08204
Alpha_k:	10.69254	15.00000	-4.30746	0.56973
Beta_k:	10.02777	10.00000	0.02777	0.56830
Phi_k:	-1.62218	5.00000	-6.62218	0.62323

Noise= .1, Deformation Model

	FIT	EXACT	ERROR	PRECISION
DeltaX_k:	5.00449	5.00000	0.00449	0.00489
DeltaY_k:	-0.02180	0.00000	-0.02180	0.00443
DeltaZ_k:	-19.97207	-20.00000	0.02793	0.01565
Alpha_k:	14.76728	15.00000	-0.23273	0.08131
Beta_k:	9.99434	10.00000	-0.00566	0.04485
Phi_k:	3.76914	5.00000	-1.23086	0.23192
BC:	0.72947	1.00000	-0.27053	0.02675
TC:	0.43569	0.50000	-0.06431	0.00564

Noise= .1, Rigid Model

	FIT	EXACT	ERROR	PRECISION

	FIT	EXACT	ERROR	PRECISION
DeltaX_k:	5.01778	5.00000	0.01778	0.05998
DeltaY_k:	0.09885	0.00000	0.09885	0.16829
DeltaZ_k:	-20.01948	-20.00000	-0.01948	0.08195
Alpha_k:	10.69851	15.00000	-4.30149	0.56911
Beta_k:	10.02623	10.00000	0.02623	0.56768
Phi_k:	-1.62005	5.00000	-6.62005	0.62255

Noise= .25, Deformation Model

	FIT	EXACT	ERROR	PRECISION
DeltaX_k:	5.00381	5.00000	0.00381	0.00532
DeltaY_k:	-0.02197	0.00000	-0.02197	0.00483
DeltaZ_k:	-19.97417	-20.00000	0.02583	0.01704
Alpha_k:	14.75756	15.00000	-0.24244	0.08854
Beta_k:	9.99125	10.00000	-0.00875	0.04883
Phi_k:	3.80120	5.00000	-1.19880	0.25243
BC:	0.73329	1.00000	-0.26671	0.02912
TC:	0.43539	0.50000	-0.06461	0.00614

Noise= .25, Rigid Model

	FIT	EXACT	ERROR	PRECISION
DeltaX_k:	5.01977	5.00000	0.01977	0.05987
DeltaY_k:	0.10484	0.00000	0.10484	0.16796
DeltaZ_k:	-20.01896	-20.00000	-0.01896	0.08182
Alpha_k:	10.70846	15.00000	-4.29154	0.56822
Beta_k:	10.02369	10.00000	0.02370	0.56679
Phi_k:	-1.61650	5.00000	-6.61650	0.62157

Noise= .5, Deformation Model

	FIT	EXACT	ERROR	PRECISION
DeltaX_k:	5.00270	5.00000	0.00270	0.00652
DeltaY_k:	-0.02224	0.00000	-0.02224	0.00592
DeltaZ_k:	-19.97765	-20.00000	0.02235	0.02088
Alpha_k:	14.74143	15.00000	-0.25857	0.10857
Beta_k:	9.98610	10.00000	-0.01390	0.05986
Phi_k:	3.85431	5.00000	-1.14569	0.30928
BC:	0.73962	1.00000	-0.26038	0.03568
TC:	0.43490	0.50000	-0.06510	0.00752

Noise= .5, Rigid Model

	FIT	EXACT	ERROR	PRECISION
DeltaX_k:	5.02308	5.00000	0.02308	0.05975
DeltaY_k:	0.11481	0.00000	0.11481	0.16755
DeltaZ_k:	-20.01809	-20.00000	-0.01809	0.08167

```
    Alpha_k:  10.72505  15.00000  -4.27495   0.56715
     Beta_k:  10.01947  10.00000   0.01947   0.56572
      Phi_k:  -1.61059   5.00000  -6.61059   0.62041
```

Noise= .75, Deformation Model

```
                FIT      EXACT     ERROR    PRECISION
   DeltaX_k:   5.00157   5.00000   0.00157   0.00807
   DeltaY_k:  -0.02252   0.00000  -0.02252   0.00733
   DeltaZ_k: -19.98118 -20.00000   0.01882   0.02588
    Alpha_k:  14.72526  15.00000  -0.27474   0.13457
     Beta_k:   9.98094  10.00000  -0.01906   0.07419
      Phi_k:   3.90825   5.00000  -1.09175   0.38306
         BC:   0.74606   1.00000  -0.25394   0.04419
         TC:   0.43441   0.50000  -0.06559   0.00932
```

Noise= .75, Rigid Model

```
                FIT      EXACT     ERROR    PRECISION
   DeltaX_k:   5.02641   5.00000   0.02641   0.05968
   DeltaY_k:   0.12452   0.00000   0.12452   0.16729
   DeltaZ_k: -20.01722 -20.00000  -0.01722   0.08159
    Alpha_k:  10.74120  15.00000  -4.25880   0.56661
     Beta_k:  10.01442  10.00000   0.01442   0.56519
      Phi_k:  -1.60509   5.00000  -6.60508   0.61982
```

Noise= 1, Deformation Model

```
                FIT      EXACT     ERROR    PRECISION
   DeltaX_k:   5.00049   5.00000   0.00049   0.00981
   DeltaY_k:  -0.02280   0.00000  -0.02280   0.00892
   DeltaZ_k: -19.98454 -20.00000   0.01546   0.03147
    Alpha_k:  14.70925  15.00000  -0.29075   0.16374
     Beta_k:   9.97586  10.00000  -0.02414   0.09025
      Phi_k:   3.95931   5.00000  -1.04069   0.46571
         BC:   0.75214   1.00000  -0.24786   0.05372
         TC:   0.43393   0.50000  -0.06607   0.01134
```

Noise= 1, Rigid Model

```
                FIT      EXACT     ERROR    PRECISION
   DeltaX_k:   5.02971   5.00000   0.02971   0.05967
   DeltaY_k:   0.13472   0.00000   0.13472   0.16718
   DeltaZ_k: -20.01636 -20.00000  -0.01636   0.08158
    Alpha_k:  10.75814  15.00000  -4.24186   0.56658
     Beta_k:  10.01099  10.00000   0.01099   0.56516
      Phi_k:  -1.59878   5.00000  -6.59878   0.61979
```

Noise= 5, Deformation Model

	FIT	EXACT	ERROR	PRECISION
DeltaX_k:	4.98367	5.00000	-0.01633	0.04130
DeltaY_k:	-0.02711	0.00000	-0.02711	0.03803
DeltaZ_k:	-20.03678	-20.00000	-0.03678	0.13375
Alpha_k:	14.45712	15.00000	-0.54289	0.69989
Beta_k:	9.89562	10.00000	-0.10438	0.38438
Phi_k:	4.75190	5.00000	-0.24810	1.96557
BC:	0.84682	1.00000	-0.15318	0.22666
TC:	0.42655	0.50000	-0.07345	0.04838

Noise= 5, Rigid Model

	FIT	EXACT	ERROR	PRECISION
DeltaX_k:	5.08221	5.00000	0.08221	0.06634
DeltaY_k:	0.29192	0.00000	0.29192	0.18466
DeltaZ_k:	-20.00261	-20.00000	-0.00261	0.09098
Alpha_k:	11.02010	15.00000	-3.97990	0.63190
Beta_k:	9.94238	10.00000	-0.05762	0.63032
Phi_k:	-1.50586	5.00000	-6.50586	0.69128

Noise= 10, Deformation Model

	FIT	EXACT	ERROR	PRECISION
DeltaX_k:	4.96475	5.00000	-0.03525	0.08052
DeltaY_k:	-0.03227	0.00000	-0.03227	0.07525
DeltaZ_k:	-20.09482	-20.00000	-0.09482	0.26348
Alpha_k:	14.15507	15.00000	-0.84493	1.38878
Beta_k:	9.79952	10.00000	-0.20048	0.75951
Phi_k:	5.62229	5.00000	0.62229	3.84175
BC:	0.95123	1.00000	-0.04877	0.44302
TC:	0.41820	0.50000	-0.08180	0.09578

Noise= 10, Rigid Model

	FIT	EXACT	ERROR	PRECISION
DeltaX_k:	5.14665	5.00000	0.14665	0.08725
DeltaY_k:	0.48419	0.00000	0.48419	0.24086
DeltaZ_k:	-19.98572	-20.00000	0.01428	0.12007
Alpha_k:	11.34189	15.00000	-3.65811	0.83407
Beta_k:	9.85707	10.00000	-0.14293	0.83201
Phi_k:	-1.39215	5.00000	-6.39215	0.91254

Noise= 25, Deformation Model

	FIT	EXACT	ERROR	PRECISION

	FIT	EXACT	ERROR	PRECISION
DeltaX_k:	4.91756	5.00000	-0.08244	0.19254
DeltaY_k:	-0.04685	0.00000	-0.04685	0.18663
DeltaZ_k:	-20.23545	-20.00000	-0.23545	0.64453
Alpha_k:	13.31776	15.00000	-1.68224	3.46643
Beta_k:	9.53157	10.00000	-0.46843	1.87462
Phi_k:	7.69098	5.00000	2.69098	9.20866
BC:	1.20212	1.00000	0.20212	1.06343
TC:	0.39737	0.50000	-0.10263	0.23788

Noise= 25, Rigid Model

	FIT	EXACT	ERROR	PRECISION
DeltaX_k:	5.33253	5.00000	0.33253	0.17191
DeltaY_k:	1.03234	0.00000	1.03234	0.46285
DeltaZ_k:	-19.93685	-20.00000	0.06315	0.23884
Alpha_k:	12.26844	15.00000	-2.73156	1.65980
Beta_k:	9.59825	10.00000	-0.40175	1.65612
Phi_k:	-1.06985	5.00000	-6.06985	1.81670

Bibliography

1. Filer, Capt Sherrie N. *Invesitgation of the Obsevability of a Satellite Cluster in a Near Circular Orbit*. MS thesis, AFIT/GA/ENY/89D-2, Graduate School of Engineering, Air Force Institute of Technology (AETC), Wright-Patterson AFB OH, December 1989 (AD-A1103970).

2. H. M. Karara, Editor-in-Chief. *Non-Topographic Photogrammetry, Second Edition*. Falls Church, VA: American Society for Photogrammetry and Remote Sensing, 1989.

3. Kreyszig, Erwin. *Advanced Engineering Mathematics, Seventh Edition*. New York: John Wiley and Sons, Inc., 1993.

4. Ruyten, Wim. Correspondence from Dr. Ruyten.

5. Ruyten, Wim. "Toward an Integrated Optical Data System for Wind Tunnel Testing." *Proceedings of the 37th AIAA Aerospace Sciences Meeting and Exhibit*. 1–11. Reston, VA: AIAA, 1999.

6. Ruyten, Wim. "Model Attitude Measurement with an Eight-Camera Pressure-Sensitive Paint System." *Proceedings of the 38th AIAA Aerospace Sciences Meeting and Exhibit*. 1–17. Reston, VA: AIAA, 2000.

7. Ruyten, Wim. "More Photogrammetry for Wind Tunnel Testing." Submitted to AIAA Journal, based on AIAA paper 2000-0831, January 2000.

8. Sellers, Marvin. *New pressure sensitive paint capability available in 16T*, found at http//www.arnold.af.mil.

9. Sellers, Marvin. *Pressure-sensitive paint technique advancements lead the way at Arnold*, found at http//www.arnold.af.mil.

10. Sizemore, Darbie. *Seeing light at the end of the wind tunnel: AEDC engineer explains technological advance in Pressure-Sensitive Paint*, found at http//www.arnold.af.mil.

11. William H. Press, Saul A. Teukolsky, William T. Vettering and Brian P. Flannery. *Numerical Recipes in Fortran, Second Edition*. New York: Cambridge University Press, 1992.

Vita

Lt Sean Krolikowski was born in Chicago, IL. After his parents divorce at the age of 3, he moved to Michigan with his mother, where they continued to move around quite a bit.

Sean graduated from Tecumseh High School in 1993, and immediately left for the United States Air Force Academy. In 1997 he graduated from the Academy with a Bachelor's of Science in Astronautical Engineering.

After his immediate commissioning, Sean recieved his first assignment at Wright-Patterson AFB in the Aeronautical Systems Center. He was assigned to the Air Superiority TPIPT of ASC/XR, development planning. There he assisted in the production of long range planning documents.

Sean received his Master's of Astronautical Engineering from AFIT in 2001. Upon graduation, he was assigned to the Space and Missile Center at Los Angeles AFB. There he will work in the Evolved Expendable Launch Vehicle (EELV) office.

REPORT DOCUMENTATION PAGE

Form Approved
OMB No. 0704-0188

The public reporting burden for this collection of information is estimated to average 1 hour per response, including the time for reviewing instructions, searching existing data sources, gathering and maintaining the data needed, and completing and reviewing the collection of information. Send comments regarding this burden estimate or any other aspect of this collection of information, including suggestions for reducing the burden, to Department of Defense, Washington Headquarters Services, Directorate for Information Operations and Reports (0704-0188), 1215 Jefferson Davis Highway, Suite 1204, Arlington, VA 22202-4302. Respondents should be aware that notwithstanding any other provision of law, no person shall be subject to any penalty for failing to comply with a collection of information if it does not display a currently valid OMB control number.
PLEASE DO NOT RETURN YOUR FORM TO THE ABOVE ADDRESS.

1. REPORT DATE (DD-MM-YYYY)	2. REPORT TYPE	3. DATES COVERED (From - To)
08-03-2001	Thesis	Mar 2000 - Mar 2001

4. TITLE AND SUBTITLE
MODIFICATION OF POSITION AND ATTITUDE DETERMINATION OF A TEST ARTICLE THROUGH PHOTOGRAMMETRY TO ACCOUNT FOR STRUCTURAL DEFORMATION

5a. CONTRACT NUMBER

5b. GRANT NUMBER

5c. PROGRAM ELEMENT NUMBER

6. AUTHOR(S)
Sean A. Krolikowski, First Lieutenant, USAF

5d. PROJECT NUMBER

5e. TASK NUMBER

5f. WORK UNIT NUMBER

7. PERFORMING ORGANIZATION NAME(S) AND ADDRESS(ES)
Air Force Institute of Technology
Graduate School of Engineering and Management
2920 P Street, Building 640
WPAFB OH 45433-7765

8. PERFORMING ORGANIZATION REPORT NUMBER
AFIT/GA/ENY/01M-03

9. SPONSORING/MONITORING AGENCY NAME(S) AND ADDRESS(ES)
AFMC/AEDC
Dr. Wim Ruyten
MS 4300
690 2nd Street
Arnold AFB, TN 37389-4300

10. SPONSOR/MONITOR'S ACRONYM(S)

11. SPONSOR/MONITOR'S REPORT NUMBER(S)

12. DISTRIBUTION/AVAILABILITY STATEMENT
APPROVED FOR PUBLIC RELEASE; DISTRIBUTION UNLIMITED

13. SUPPLEMENTARY NOTES

14. ABSTRACT
This study improved the current method of position and attitude determination to account for structural deformation of the wind tunnel test article due to aerodynamic loading. To account for deformation, parabolic bending and linear twisting coefficients were added into the Levenberg-Marquardt multi-paramter solver. By accounting for deformation, the accuracy of position and attitude determination was greatly improved. This study also takes a qualitative look at the optimum number of wind tunnel cameras and model targets. Optimal configuration was found to be around 50 targets and 2 cameras offset by 90 degrees.

15. SUBJECT TERMS
Structural Deformation, Levenberg-Marquardt, Position and Attitude Determination

16. SECURITY CLASSIFICATION OF:			17. LIMITATION OF ABSTRACT	18. NUMBER OF PAGES	19a. NAME OF RESPONSIBLE PERSON
a. REPORT	b. ABSTRACT	c. THIS PAGE	UU	107	Dr. Steven G. Tragesser, AFIT/ENY
U	U	U			19b. TELEPHONE NUMBER (Include area code) (937)255-6565 x4326

Standard Form 298 (Rev. 8/98)
Prescribed by ANSI Std. Z39.18

CPSIA information can be obtained
at www.ICGtesting.com
Printed in the USA
BVHW011301130520
579640BV00007B/91